ENERGY
BALLS

ENERGY
BALLS

Improve your
physical performance,
mental focus, sleep,
mood, and more!

CHRISTAL SCZEBEL, C. H. N.

CHRONICLE BOOKS

SAN FRANCISCO

Library of Congress Cataloging-in-Publication Data:

Names: Sczebel, Christal, author.
Title: Energy balls / by Christal Sczebel.
Description: San Francisco : Chronicle Books, [2016] |
Includes index.
Identifiers: LCCN 2016026958 | ISBN 9781452158884
(pb : alk. paper)
Subjects: LCSH: Cooking (Nuts) | Snack foods. | Gluten-free
diet—Recipes. |
  LCGFT: Cookbooks.
Classification: LCC TX814 .S435 2016 | DDC 641.6/45—dc23
LC record available at https://lccn.loc.gov/2016026958

Manufactured in China

Editorial Director: Ellen Dupont
Associate Publisher: Sarah Bloxham
Project Editor: Julie Booke
Proofreader: Marion Dent
Designer: Leah Germann
Food styling and photography: Christal Sczebel

10 9 8 7 6 5 4 3 2 1

Chronicle books and gifts are available at special quantity
discounts to corporations, professional associations, literacy
programs, and other organizations. For details and discount
information, please contact our corporate/premiums
department at corporatesales@chroniclebooks.com or at
1-800-759-0190.

Chronicle Books LLC
680 Second Street
San Francisco, California 94107
www.chroniclebooks.com

Contents

Foreword

What happens when you take wonderful whole-food, energy-boosting ingredients, whirl them together in a food processor, and then roll them together lovingly with your hands? You'll have made a simple, convenient, pop-in-your-mouth, flavorful energy ball to enhance your stamina and put a little pep in your step.

When it comes to snacks, there are plenty of options, but they may not be as healthy as they appear. Granola bars can be chock-full of refined sugars, crackers are sometimes filled with hydrogenated oils, and some fruit snacks have barely a hint of real fruit in them! With so many options, it can be confusing to know what to choose to fuel your body.

As a nutritionist, people often ask me to recommend convenient snacks that will ward off cravings, hunger pangs, and energy slumps. Energy balls are the answer. These snacks are quick and fun to make and easy to store and carry; plus, they taste amazing.

We all have busy lives and need the right fuel to give our brains and bodies a steady stream of energy throughout the day. Energy balls fit the bill at any time. Whether it's a couple of breakfast balls in the morning, a lunch-box ball at midday, a brain-boosting ball when you need extra mental stamina, a performance-enhancing ball for sports, or a bedtime ball to increase libido or promote calming energy in the evening, there's one to suit your needs.

The ingredients you use to make the energy balls in this book are superior to any packaged or processed snack. They contain raw nuts, seeds, dried fruits, superfoods, nut flours, nutritional powders, whole grains, and more. All of these are unrefined, natural, and provide ample amounts of vitamins, minerals, healthy fats, proteins, and slow-release carbohydrates for sustained energy.

By eating these foods, you can cut out the refined sugars, artificial colors and flavors, and sweeteners found in other snacks that will decrease your energy. Refined and artificial ingredients place a toxic load on the body, forcing it to work even harder to rid them from our system. This in turn essentially robs our bodies of energy, leaving us with that sluggish feeling and those dreaded "crashes."

While making homemade snacks might not sound like the most efficient route, once you have made your first batch of energy balls, you'll realize just how easy they are—and after one bite, you'll be hooked! So what are you waiting for? It's time to learn how to boost your energy naturally with 100 delicious energy balls.

Basic Ingredients

The following ingredients are the building blocks for creating energy balls that are nutrient-rich, hold together well, and have a nice chewy texture.

Almonds

Almonds are rich in magnesium, calcium, and iron, and are a source of healthy unsaturated fats. They create texture, add bulk, and, thanks to the healthy fats they contain, make you feel full.

Almond Butter

This rich, velvety paste has all the benefits of almonds and adds moisture and richness. Choose a natural butter that contains only almonds to avoid the sugars and oils added to some butters.

Almond Flour or Meal (Ground Almonds)

Use almond flour in energy balls for a softer, chewier consistency. It adds bulk and healthy fats, and blends well with dried fruit.

Almond Milk

Almond milk adds moisture to energy balls and helps to bind the ingredients together. Always buy unsweetened almond milk. If you do not like almond milk, or need to avoid it, substitute another nondairy milk, such as oat, soy, rice, flax, hemp, or coconut milk.

Brown Rice Syrup

This unrefined sweetener is a great alternative to regular sugars. A great vegan alternative to honey, it is a source of manganese, iron, potassium, and magnesium.

Cacao Powder (Raw) and Cocoa Powder

Raw cacao powder is made from cacao beans. The fat is removed through a process that keeps the nutrients intact. Cocoa powder is produced from roasted cacao beans and may have lost some

Almonds

nutrients. You can substitute cocoa powder for raw cacao powder. Both contain magnesium, iron, calcium, and vitamin B_6.

Cashews

Raw cashews contain healthy unsaturated fats, protein, and carbohydrates and are a source of magnesium, iron, and vitamin B_6. In energy balls, they create a crunchy texture and add bulk.

Coconut

Shredded unsweetened coconut is rich in fats and fiber, and adds bulk and flavor. Unlike dried or desiccated coconut, it increases the moisture content of energy balls. It contains vitamins C and E, B vitamins, iron, selenium, calcium, magnesium, and phosphorus.

Coconut Flour

Coconut flour contains all the nutrients and benefits of shredded coconut, but three times the fiber and about one-quarter of the fat. In an energy ball, it soaks up moisture and creates a light, fluffy, cakelike consistency. Look for products without any additives.

Coconut Nectar

An alternative to sugar, coconut nectar is made from the sap of coconut palm tree flowers. It is low glycemic and releases slowly into the bloodstream. Alternatively, you can use agave nectar, which is derived from the sap of the agave plant. This sweetener is controversial as it is said to contain excessive amounts of fructose, which can negatively affect blood-sugar levels. While agave nectar may not be ideal, in my opinion it is superior to refined sugar. Use honey in place of coconut or agave nectar for a nonvegan option.

Coconut Palm Sugar

When compared to refined sugars, coconut palm sugar is low on the glycemic index, meaning it releases more slowly into the bloodstream. It contains trace amounts of vitamin C, potassium, phosphorous, magnesium, calcium, zinc, iron, and copper, which makes it nutritionally superior to refined granulated sugars.

Cashews

Cocoa powder

Dark Chocolate

While cocoa and cacao powder bring a chocolate flavor to energy balls, sometimes you need the real thing. Dark chocolate is rich in antioxidants, has the same nutritional benefits as cocoa and cacao powder, and varieties that contain at least 70 percent cacao have a reduced sugar content and higher overall nutritional value. To check that a chocolate is suitable for a vegan diet, make sure it does not contain modified milk or dairy products.

Dates

Pitted dates are naturally sweet and have a low glycemic load, meaning that they don't cause a spike in blood-sugar levels. Dates are a source of magnesium, calcium, iron, phosphorus, potassium, zinc, vitamins A and K, and several B vitamins. They work best when they are soft and moist. If your dates have dried out, soak them in hot water for 10 to 15 minutes, then drain before use.

Maple Syrup, Pure

This ingredient is near and dear to my heart, as it is of Canadian origin. Pure maple syrup contains manganese, zinc, calcium, iron, potassium, and magnesium, and, as a natural sweetener, it releases more slowly into the bloodstream than sugar, preventing blood sugar spikes. It is found in two grades: Grade A, Amber Color and Rich Flavor and Grade A, Dark Color and Robust Flavor. I suggest the Grade A Amber for its rich taste with balanced medium levels in flavor and color. Do not use imitation maple syrups.

Oats, Gluten-Free Rolled

These rolled seeds are bursting with B vitamins, iron, magnesium, fiber, and slow-release complex carbohydrates. In some recipes they are replaced with quick oats, as those blend better to provide bulk without a grainy texture. Always use certified gluten-free plain, unsweetened oats.

Maple syrup

Oats

Tools and Techniques

While some energy balls can be made by hand in a bowl, most need to be made with a food processor. All the other equipment you need is commonly found in the kitchen.

Essential Tools

Multispeed Food Processor

A food processor is the ultimate tool when it comes to blending nuts, seeds, and dried fruit, but you don't need anything fancy. Choose one that holds at least 12 cups (2.8 L) and has low, high, and pulse speeds. You can use a high-speed blender instead, but as the base is narrower, it is likely you will need to blend the ingredients in smaller batches, then mix them together in a bowl.

Large Mixing Bowl

This will give you more room to work, rather than trying to mix ingredients in the bowl of the food processor.

Large Plates or Small Baking Sheets

A flat work surface is essential for rolling balls in a coating and holding them for a stint in the refrigerator or freezer. Just make sure the plate or pan you use fits easily in your refrigerator or freezer.

Spatula

Energy-ball batter can get pretty sticky. Use a spatula to scrape the sides of the food processor or bowl to make sure all the ingredients come together into one large portion of batter.

Refrigerator and Freezer

Energy balls are best when given around 30 minutes to "set" in the refrigerator or freezer. This allows the ingredients to really meld together and creates a firmer consistency and texture.

Techniques

Processing

Most recipes begin by processing the ingredients on high, as this helps to incorporate them. Once the ingredients have been processed into smaller pieces, working them at a low speed helps to bind the batter together. Liquids such as almond milk can be added at this final, low speed to create a sticky, moldable batter.

Shaping

When it comes to shaping the batter into balls, most often you use your hands. Sometimes your hands should be slightly wet, as this will prevent the batter from sticking to them as you roll it into a ball shape. Roll the balls in the palms of your hands and don't be afraid to use a firm pressure to get the ball to stay in shape. Use a tablespoon measure to scoop the batter, or do it by eye.

Coating

Some recipes call for a special coating, such as a chocolate shell, grated citrus zest, cinnamon sugar, rolled oats, chopped nuts, or seeds. Spread dry coatings over a plate and roll the ball gently in the coating, then place the ball on a separate plate. To coat an energy ball in a liquid such as melted chocolate, using a toothpick or skewer to hold the ball, dip it into the liquid, lift out, and slowly rotate it as the coating hardens. A cold energy ball always coats better than a room-temperature ball, so make sure that the energy balls have been adequately chilled before coating.

Storage

Each recipe indicates the ideal way to store the energy balls for best consistency, but as a general rule, they can be stored in an airtight container in the refrigerator for up to 2 weeks, or in the freezer for up to 2 months (but let them thaw at room temperature for 10 to 15 minutes before eating). Most can be stored at room temperature, but then consume within 5 days.

Special Diets

All the energy balls in this book are suitable for vegan diets, and are gluten, egg, soy, and dairy free.

Diabetes/Low-Glycemic Diet

A diet specific for diabetics, or a low-glycemic diet, is focused on foods that do not greatly affect circulating glucose levels, and it is important to be mindful of the amount of sugar in specific foods. While dried fruits, and dates in particular, are low in carbohydrates, they do have a higher sugar content. However, when it comes to glycemic index, dates fall in the lower range and therefore diabetics can eat dates in small amounts. One benefit of energy balls is that they contain fat- and protein-rich ingredients that act to slow the release of the sugar into the bloodstream. For diabetics or anyone following a low-glycemic-index diet, I recommend consuming no more than one energy ball at a time, and no more than three per day, but consult your doctor before adding energy balls to your diet.

Grain-free

A grain-free diet eliminates all grains—the seeds of plants such as wheat, oats, and rice. Replace the oats with an equal amount of a grain-free flour, such as almond. No substitutions can be made for the Cocoa Crispy Rice and the Sweet-and-Salty Popcorn balls.

Paleolithic/Primal

The Paleolithic, or Paleo, diet excludes dairy (the Primal diet allows some raw, fermented dairy products), grains, and processed foods. For a Paleo diet, use the grain-free variations, and use maple syrup or coconut nectar rather than agave nectar. For a strict Paleo diet, substitute an unsweetened baking chocolate for 70 percent dark chocolate. As legumes are not allowed on a Paleo diet, replace peanuts with almonds or cashews; the Vanilla Cake Balls are not suitable, as there is no substitute for chickpeas.

Peanut/Nut-free

While many of the energy balls in this book contain nuts, others are nut-free because they use seeds and seed butter. You can replace the peanuts or peanut butter with the same amount of almonds or cashews and almond or cashew butter.

Pregnancy

Energy balls are fantastic to enjoy during pregnancy, as they are made with whole-food ingredients and provide fiber, protein, and healthy fats. Many of the ingredients found in these energy balls, such as oats, bananas, nuts and nut butters, and figs, are specifically helpful during pregnancy.

Soy-free

Some protein powders contain soy, so if you are following a soy-free diet, look for a protein powder made with hemp, brown rice, or pea protein.

[Breakfast
Energy Balls]

Energy balls made with slow-releasing complex
carbohydrates, including whole grains and cereals,
are ideal at breakfast time. This chapter contains
delicious, easy recipes made with vitamin-rich fruits,
such as lemon, peach, and blueberry, and fiber-rich
seeds including chia and flax. All of these whole-food
ingredients provide energy and give the digestive
system a helping hand, making them a great option
to enjoy as the day begins.

Active Ingredients

Apples

Apples are one of my favorite fruits, and this chapter uses them fresh and dried. They provide fiber and vitamin C, which support the adrenal glands. These glands help to regulate stress hormones and keep energy levels stable. The fiber will ward off hunger.

Blueberries

Dried blueberries are incredibly rich in dietary fiber, are a source of calcium and vitamin A, and have a soft, chewy consistency similar to that of a raisin. Look for berries that have been sun-dried and do not contain added sweeteners, oil, or sulfur dioxide. The fiber in blueberries helps to boost digestion at breakfast time.

Chia Seeds

"Chia" means strength, and these seeds are often used to boost energy. They can be black or white, and have a similar texture to poppy seeds. When added to liquids, chia seeds create a gel-like consistency, making them a great food for digestion. They are full of fiber and rich in manganese, calcium, zinc, and phosphorus. The fiber boosts digestion and helps to satisfy the appetite.

Cinnamon

Fragrant cinnamon has a host of benefits, including blood sugar stabilization and heart disease prevention. It contains antioxidants, calcium, manganese, iron, and fiber. It wakes up the metabolism, so its wonderful flavor enhances many common breakfast foods.

Flaxseed, Ground (Flax Meal)

Flaxseed, also known as linseed, is incredibly nutritious. Historically, these seeds were used as a laxative, and in a breakfast ball they stimulate and support digestion. They are rich in fiber, magnesium, calcium, vitamin B_6, and iron.

Granola

I use gluten-free vegan granola to provide a crunchy texture and sweet, toasted flavor. It is rich in fiber and slow-releasing carbohydrates for sustained energy from the oats, and healthful fats from the nuts. Granola is typically rich in magnesium, iron, and B vitamins. Some granola is loaded with sweetener, so look for one with less than 6 g of sugar per ¼ cup (30 g) serving.

Cinnamon

Lemons

Lemon adds a tart, citrus twist and naturally stimulates the production of digestive enzymes, which is why a glass of lemon water is a great idea in the morning. Lemons are also loaded with vitamin C, which helps to support immunity and overall health. Consumed at breakfast, lemon helps ensure good digestive function throughout the day.

Maple Sugar

Maple sugar is a granulated form of pure maple syrup (see page 10). It is similar in flavor to pure maple syrup and works nicely as a granulated sugar coating. Maple sugar contains manganese, zinc, calcium, potassium, iron, and magnesium. Unlike the refined sugar you'll find in breakfast cereals or sweetened oatmeals, it releases slowly into the bloodstream.

Maple sugar

Peaches

Dried peaches are moist, chewy, and soft and add texture to energy balls as well as acting as a binder. Dried peaches are rich in vitamins A, K, B_2, and B_3—which help to stimulate energy and alertness—as well as iron, copper, potassium, and manganese. They contain energy-boosting goodness in the form of carbohydrates. Look for dried fruit that does not contain sulfur dioxide.

Pecans

Raw pecans are a source of healthy unsaturated fats and provide bulk and delicious taste to recipes. Crunchy and rich, they are a great combination with rolled oats and maple syrup. They contain magnesium, manganese, phosphorus, and iron; vitamins B_2 and B_6; and healthy fats, protein, and carbohydrates. The omega fatty acids will help to ward off hunger and keep you feeling full.

Raisins

Raisins are a source of manganese, copper, potassium, B vitamins, and vitamin C. They are also a great source of fiber, and thus are a wonderful addition to breakfast balls for boosting digestion. They increase energy as well, thanks to the carbohydrates they contain. Raisins have a sticky and chewy consistency that works to bind together ball ingredients and create a soft, chewy texture. Avoid golden raisins that have been treated with sulfur dioxide.

Pecans

Banana Bread

If you love banana bread, you'll love these light, breadlike energy balls. Whole, naturally dried bananas are mixed with peanut butter, dates, whole almonds, almond flour, pumpkin-seed protein powder, natural raw cacao nibs, and a splash of unsweetened almond milk. Adding nut flour and protein powder to the carbohydrates in the dried fruit and the fats in the nuts and nut butter create a perfectly balanced snack to kick-start your day.

MAKES 12 BALLS

3 dried whole bananas, chopped into pieces

½ cup [80 g] pitted dates

½ cup [80 g] natural pumpkin-seed protein powder

¼ cup [30 g] almond meal or ground almonds

¼ cup [35 g] raw almonds

¼ cup [65 g] natural peanut butter or almond butter

4 Tbsp [30 g] natural raw cacao nibs

¼ cup [60 ml] unsweetened almond milk

1 In a food processor, combine the bananas, dates, protein powder, almond meal, whole almonds, peanut butter, and 2 Tbsp of the cacao nibs and process on high for 1 to 2 minutes.

2 Reduce the speed to low and pour the almond milk through the top opening as you continue to process the mixture for about 1 minute, until a sticky mass forms.

3 Spread the remaining 2 Tbsp cacao nibs on a large plate. Using a tablespoon, scoop the mixture and, with clean slightly wet hands, shape the mixture into a ball between your palms.

4 Roll the ball in the cacao nibs to lightly coat, and set on a separate plate. Repeat with the remaining mixture until you have 12 balls slightly smaller than a golf ball.

5 Place the balls in the freezer to set for 1 to 2 hours. Store in an airtight container in the refrigerator or at room temperature until required.

SERVING SIZE: 1 BALL	
Calories	90
Protein	3 g
Fat	3 g
Carbohydrate	13 g
Sugar	9 g
Dietary fiber	2 g
Vitamins	B_6
Minerals	iron, magnesium, potassium

Try this!
Banana–Walnut Bread
Omit the almond meal and raw almonds, and replace with the same amount of walnut meal or ground walnuts and ¼ cup [30 g] raw walnuts.

Banana–Coconut Bread
Omit the almond meal, raw almonds, and cacao nibs, and replace with ¼ cup [25 g] coconut flour and ¼ cup [20 g] lightly toasted unsweetened shredded coconut. Coat the balls with another ¼ cup [20 g] lightly toasted shredded unsweetened coconut.

Apple Pie and Almond Butter

MAKES 18 BALLS

1 cup [160 g] pitted dates

1 cup [60 g] dried unsweetened apple rings

1 small Gala apple, cored and finely chopped

½ cup [70 g] raw almonds

¼ cup [30 g] vegan vanilla protein powder

2 Tbsp raw almond butter

1 Tbsp ground cinnamon

¼ tsp ground nutmeg

¼ cup [25 g] gluten-free rolled oats

1 tsp organic coconut palm sugar

Combine the classic flavor of apple pie with almond butter to give your body a wake-up call! Dried, unsweetened apple rings—blended with fresh apple, dates, whole almonds, almond butter, vanilla protein powder, cinnamon, and nutmeg—pack a healthy punch. Cinnamon is a natural metabolism booster; combined with the slow-release carbohydrates from the oats, these balls will give you sustained energy all morning. Coconut palm sugar releases slowly into the bloodstream, preventing a spike in blood sugar that might cause an afternoon crash.

1 In a food processor, combine the dates, apple rings, chopped apple, whole almonds, protein powder, almond butter, cinnamon, and nutmeg and process on high for 3 to 5 minutes, until a sticky mass forms.

2 Spread the oats and coconut palm sugar on a large plate. Line a baking sheet with wax or parchment paper. Using a tablespoon, scoop the mixture and, with clean slightly wet hands, shape the mixture into a ball between your palms.

3 Roll the ball in the oats and sugar to lightly coat, and set on the prepared baking sheet. Repeat with the remaining mixture until you have 18 balls slightly smaller than a golf ball.

4 Place the balls in the freezer to set for 30 minutes. Store in an airtight container in the refrigerator until required.

Try this!
Salted Apple Pie

Omit the protein powder and replace with the ¼ cup [25 g] of rolled oats used for coating the balls. Add ½ tsp kosher salt to the food processor with the rest of the ingredients for a sweet-and-salty flavor combination. Roll in 1 tsp ground cinnamon.

SERVING SIZE: 1 BALL	
Calories	90
Protein	3 g
Fat	3 g
Carbohydrate	13 g
Sugar	9 g
Dietary fiber	2 g
Vitamins	all B's, C, E
Minerals	calcium, magnesium, phosphorus, zinc

If the dates look dry, place them in warm water. Set aside for 10 to 15 minutes, until softened, then drain.

Maple, Pecan, and Oatmeal

MAKES 18 BALLS

2 cups [200 g] gluten-free rolled oats

1 cup [120 g] chopped or crushed raw pecans

¼ cup [40 g] ground flaxseed

2 Tbsp pure maple sugar

pinch of salt

½ cup [130 g] almond butter

¼ cup [60 ml] pure maple syrup

¼ cup [60 ml] brown rice syrup

It's no wonder that oatmeal is a breakfast staple, as it's full of B vitamins and fiber. This recipe combines the goodness of oats with pecans, which are rich in manganese, copper, and zinc, as well as healthy dietary fats. As a bonus, the pure maple syrup contains calcium, while the fiber in the flaxseed aids digestion. The fiber, fats, protein, and slow-release complex carbohydrates will help to keep you satisfied from breakfast until it's time for a morning snack.

1 Combine the oats, pecans, flaxseed, maple sugar, and salt in a bowl. Add the almond butter, maple syrup, and brown rice syrup to the bowl and mix until a sticky mass forms.

2 Using a tablespoon, scoop the mixture and, with clean slightly wet hands, shape the mixture into a ball between your palms, then set on a plate. Repeat with the remaining mixture until you have 18 balls, each just smaller than a golf ball.

3 Place the balls in the freezer to set for 30 minutes. Store in an airtight container in the refrigerator until required.

Try this!

Maple, Pecan, Hemp, and Oatmeal

Add protein and extra magnesium by adding 2 heaping Tbsp hemp hearts to the bowl with the oats, pecans, flaxseed, maple sugar, and salt.

SERVING SIZE: 1 BALL	
Calories	154
Protein	4 g
Fat	9 g
Carbohydrate	16 g
Sugar	6 g
Dietary fiber	3 g
Vitamins	All B's, E
Minerals	calcium, copper, iron, magnesium, manganese, zinc

To prevent
the mixture from
sticking to your hands,
rinse with water and pat
dry slightly after
making two or
three balls.

Cranberry-Chocolate Granola

Granola bars are a grab-and-go option for those who want a morning snack or easy breakfast—but they aren't all created equal. Many processed bars are full of artificial ingredients and loaded with sweeteners. These delicious balls are full of whole foods, natural slow-release sugar, protein, healthy fats, and dietary fiber. Look for an organic granola that is naturally sweetened, free of refined sugars, and contains less than ¼ oz [7 g] of sugar per serving. Two of these balls at breakfast will keep you energized and feeling satisfied—with no energy crash.

MAKES 14 BALLS

1 cup [160 g] pitted dates

1 cup [140 g] raw almonds

½ cup [60 g] dried unsweetened cranberries, plus 2 Tbsp chopped

1 cup [110 g] granola

¼ cup [60 ml] unsweetened almond milk

2 Tbsp finely chopped 70% cacao solids vegan dark chocolate

1 In a food processor, combine the dates, almonds, ½ cup [60 g] dried cranberries, and ½ cup [55 g] of the granola and process on low for 30 seconds, then on high for about 30 seconds longer, until combined. Reduce the speed to low, pour in the almond milk, and process for 1 to 2 minutes, until a sticky mass forms.

2 Transfer the mixture to a large bowl and fold in the chopped dried cranberries and chopped dark chocolate.

3 Spread the remaining ½ cup [55 g] granola on a large plate. Using a tablespoon, scoop the mixture and, with clean slightly wet hands, shape the mixture into a ball between your palms. Roll the ball in the granola to lightly coat, and set on a separate plate. Repeat with the remaining mixture until you have 14 balls, each just smaller than a golf ball.

4 Place the balls in the freezer to set for 30 minutes. Store in an airtight container in the refrigerator, or at room temperature if you prefer a softer consistency, until required.

Try this!
Goji Berry Granola

To add the antioxidant power of goji berries, replace the ½ cup [60 g] dried cranberries with ½ cup [55 g] dried goji berries. If your goji are dry, soak them in hot water for 5 minutes, drain, then blend with the remaining ingredients.

SERVING SIZE: 1 BALL	
Calories	143
Protein	3 g
Fat	6 g
Carbohydrate	21 g
Sugar	14 g
Dietary fiber	3 g
Vitamins	All B's, C, E
Minerals	copper, iron, magnesium, manganese, phosphorous

Lemon, Almond, and Chia Muffin

MAKES 12 BALLS

1 cup [140 g] raw cashews

1 cup [160 g] pitted dates

½ cup [60 g] almond meal or flour or ground almonds, plus 1 Tbsp

2 Tbsp coconut flour

2 Tbsp chia seeds

3 Tbsp finely grated lemon zest

1 Tbsp fresh lemon juice

1 Tbsp coconut or agave nectar

½ tsp pure almond extract

¼ tsp pure lemon extract

¼ tsp pure vanilla extract

1 Tbsp unsweetened almond milk

Lemon juice naturally stimulates the production of digestive enzymes, which is why starting your day with a glass of lemon water is a great way to aid digestion. These balls combine the power of lemons with fiber-rich chia seeds and mineral-rich almonds, cashews, coconut flour, and dates. This combination makes for a light, muffinlike taste and texture that hits any real muffin out of the park when it comes to nutrition. Many muffins are loaded with saturated fats, refined sugar, and calories, so a couple of these balls are a healthy alternative in the morning.

1 In a food processor, combine the cashews, dates, ½ cup [60 g] almond meal, coconut flour, 1 Tbsp of the chia seeds, 1 Tbsp of the lemon zest, the lemon juice, the coconut nectar, and the extracts and process on high for about 30 seconds, until combined. Reduce the speed to low, pour in the almond milk, and process for about 30 seconds, until a sticky and slightly crumbly mass forms.

2 Transfer the mixture to a large bowl and fold in 1 Tbsp of the remaining lemon zest.

3 Using a tablespoon, scoop the mixture and, with clean slightly wet hands, shape the mixture into a ball between your palms, then set on a plate. Repeat with the remaining mixture until you have 12 balls slightly smaller than a golf ball. Sprinkle the balls with the remaining 1 Tbsp lemon zest and 1 Tbsp chia seeds.

4 Place the balls in the freezer to set for 30 minutes. Store in an airtight container in the refrigerator or at room temperature until required.

Try this!

Lemon–Poppy Seed Muffin

Lemon and poppy seeds are a classic combination, and the seeds add calcium, magnesium, and iron to any dish. Simply replace the 1 Tbsp chia seeds in the energy balls with 1 Tbsp poppy seeds, and the 1 Tbsp chia seeds in the coating with 1 Tbsp poppy seeds.

SERVING SIZE: 1 BALL	
Calories	143
Protein	4 g
Fat	7 g
Carbohydrate	17 g
Sugar	11 g
Dietary fiber	3 g
Vitamins	B₁, B₂, B₆, C, E, K
Minerals	copper, iron, magnesium, manganese, phosphorus

Use a muffin
or cupcake pan to
hold energy balls while
they set in the freezer,
or to store them before
you eat them.

Cinnamon-Raisin

Everyone loves the aroma of cinnamon, but it does more than just smell delicious—it also contains calcium and iron for strong bones, and it will boost your metabolism and immunity. Here, the cinnamon is combined with naturally sweet raisins and dates, as well as almonds, which are a great source of omega-rich fats, protein, vitamins, and minerals. These energy balls are a healthy alternative to cinnamon–raisin toast, as they will get you going in the morning and keep you energized.

MAKES 12 BALLS

1 cup [140 g] raw almonds

½ cup [70 g] dark raisins

½ cup [80 g] pitted dates

½ cup [60 g] almond meal or flour or ground almonds

2 Tbsp unsweetened almond milk

1 Tbsp ground cinnamon

1 Tbsp coconut palm sugar

1 Combine the whole almonds, raisins, dates, almond meal, almond milk, ½ Tbsp of the cinnamon, and ½ Tbsp of the coconut palm sugar in a food processor and process on high for about 1 minute, until a sticky mass forms. You can process the mixture longer for a smoother mixture, or for a shorter time for a chunkier mixture.

2 Combine the remaining ½ Tbsp cinnamon and ½ Tbsp coconut palm sugar in a small bowl. Using a tablespoon, scoop the raisin mixture and, with clean slightly wet hands, shape the mixture into a ball between your palms. Roll the ball in the cinnamon and coconut palm sugar to lightly coat, and set on a plate. Repeat with the remaining mixture until you have 12 balls, each just smaller than a golf ball.

3 Place the balls in the freezer to set for 30 minutes. Store in an airtight container in the refrigerator or at room temperature until required.

Try this!
Cinnamon-Raisin-Walnut
Add the rich, unctuous flavor of walnuts by replacing the 1 cup [140 g] raw almonds with 1 cup [120 g] raw walnuts.

SERVING SIZE: 1 BALL	
Calories	139
Protein	3 g
Fat	8 g
Carbohydrate	15 g
Sugar	10 g
Dietary fiber	3 g
Vitamins	B₂, B₆, E
Minerals	copper, iron, magnesium, manganese, potassium

Blueberry Muffin

Muffins are a popular breakfast choice, but they are not always the healthiest option, as they can be packed with saturated fats and refined sugars. These energy balls celebrate the classic muffin, with added nutrients in each bite! Cashews, almond meal, coconut flour, pitted dates, dried blueberries, and the natural sweetness of coconut or agave nectar and coconut palm sugar create a delicious replica of a blueberry muffin in a ball that is rich in fiber, healthy fats, and slower-releasing carbohydrates; and these give a hit of protein, too.

MAKES 12 BALLS

½ cup [80 g] pitted dates

½ cup [80 g] dried unsweetened blueberries

½ cup [70 g] raw cashews

½ cup [60 g] almond meal or flour or ground almonds

½ cup [50 g] coconut flour

2 Tbsp coconut or agave nectar

½ tsp pure vanilla extract

¼ cup [60 ml] unsweetened almond milk

1 tsp coconut palm sugar (optional)

1 Combine the dates, blueberries, cashews, almond meal, coconut flour, coconut nectar, and vanilla in a food processor and process on high for about 30 seconds, until combined. Reduce the speed to low, pour in the almond milk, and process for about 30 seconds longer until a sticky but slightly crumbly mass forms.

2 Using a tablespoon, scoop the mixture and, with clean slightly wet hands, shape the mixture into a ball between your palms, then set on a plate. Repeat with the remaining mixture until you have 12 balls, each just smaller than a golf ball. Sprinkle the balls with the coconut palm sugar, if you like.

3 Place the balls in the freezer to set for 30 minutes. Store in an airtight container in the refrigerator or at room temperature until required.

Try this!
Lemon–Blueberry Muffin

Lemon and blueberry make a great flavor combination, and lemon adds a little dose of vitamin C. Add 1 Tbsp fresh lemon juice, 1 Tbsp finely grated lemon zest, and ¼ tsp pure lemon extract with the other ingredients.

SERVING SIZE: 1 BALL	
Calories	125
Protein	3 g
Fat	5 g
Carbohydrate	17 g
Sugar	11 g
Dietary fiber	4 g
Vitamins	B_2, B_6, C, K, E
Minerals	copper, magnesium, manganese, phosphorus, selenium

Peach Cobbler

Who says you can't have dessert for breakfast? Peach cobbler may be an unusual breakfast dish, but the oats and peaches it contains are both healthy. Thanks to the oats, which are rich in fiber and B vitamins, these balls are sure to keep you feeling full and energized. The dried peaches add a delicious fruit flavor, vitamins A and C, and natural sweetness. The raw nuts contain healthy fats, while the coconut palm sugar increases the sweetness, but—as it is low on the glycemic index—it won't lead to a spike in blood sugar levels.

MAKES 12 BALLS

1½ cups [270 g] dried unsweetened peach halves

1 cup [140 g] raw cashews

½ cup [60 g] almond meal or flour or ground almonds

½ cup [50 g] gluten-free rolled oats

1 tsp ground cinnamon

1 tsp coconut palm sugar

½ tsp pure vanilla extract

2 Tbsp unsweetened almond milk

1 Combine the peaches, cashews, almond meal, oats, cinnamon, coconut palm sugar, and vanilla in a food processor and process on high for about 1 minute, until finely ground (do not worry if some larger chunks of dried peach remain).

2 Reduce the speed to low, pour in the almond milk, and process for about 30 seconds, until a sticky mass forms.

3 Using a tablespoon, scoop the mixture and, with clean slightly wet hands, shape the mixture into a ball between your palms, then set on a plate. Repeat with the remaining mixture until you have 12 balls, each just smaller than a golf ball.

4 Place the balls in the freezer to set for 30 minutes. Store in an airtight container in the refrigerator or at room temperature until required.

Try this!

Protein Peach Cobbler

Increasing the protein in these balls will help to keep your blood sugar level and your energy up. Replace the ½ cup [60 g] almond meal with ½ cup [60 g] vegan vanilla protein powder. Because the protein powder should be naturally sweetened, you can omit the 1 tsp coconut palm sugar, if you wish. As some protein powders are more absorbent than others, you may need a little more unsweetened almond milk to achieve the desired consistency.

SERVING SIZE: 1 BALL	
Calories	123
Protein	4 g
Fat	7 g
Carbohydrate	13 g
Sugar	7 g
Dietary fiber	2 g
Vitamins	A, all B's, C, K
Minerals	copper, iron, magnesium, manganese, phosphorus

Raisin-Bran

This delicious twist on a classic breakfast dish contains all the flavors, texture, and fiber of raisins and bran. Thanks to this combination of simple, healthy ingredients, the balls give a steady supply of energy. Oat bran and ground flaxseed add fiber and slow-releasing carbohydrates, as well as B vitamins. The raisins, dates, and coconut palm sugar add a natural sweetness to round out the fiber-rich bran flavor. Dipped in almond milk, these balls will make you think of the classic breakfast cereal, but with even more nutritious punch packed into every bite.

MAKES 12 BALLS

1½ cups [210 g] dark raisins

10 pitted dates

1 cup [95 g] gluten-free oat bran

¼ cup [40 g] ground flaxseed

2 Tbsp coconut palm sugar

2 Tbsp unsweetened almond milk

1 Combine the raisins, dates, oat bran, flaxseed, and 1 Tbsp of the coconut palm sugar in a food processor and process on low for 30 seconds. Scrape the sides of the bowl with a plastic spatula and process again. Pour in the almond milk and process for about 30 seconds longer, until a mass starts to form.

2 Spread the remaining 1 Tbsp coconut palm sugar on a plate.

3 Using a tablespoon, scoop the mixture and, with clean slightly wet hands, shape the mixture into a ball between your palms. Roll the ball in the coconut palm sugar to lightly coat, and set on a separate plate. Repeat with the remaining mixture until you have 12 balls, each just smaller than a golf ball.

4 Place the balls in the freezer to set for 30 minutes. Store in an airtight container in the refrigerator, or at room temperature if you prefer a softer consistency, until required.

Try this!

Banana, Cinnamon, and Raisin-Bran

A sliced banana and a pinch of cinnamon are a great way to add more flavor and nutrition to a bowl of raisin bran. Here's how to achieve it in energy-ball form: Reduce the raisins to 1 cup [140 g] and the dates to 5, then add ¾ cup [65 g] chopped dehydrated banana pieces (not banana chips) and 1 tsp ground cinnamon.

SERVING SIZE: 1 BALL	
Calories	132
Protein	3 g
Fat	2 g
Carbohydrate	29 g
Sugar	17 g
Dietary fiber	4 g
Vitamins	A, all B's
Minerals	iron, manganese, potassium

Lunch-Box
Energy Balls

Enjoy energy balls based on lunchtime classics for tasty recipes and meals that are fun. These lunch-box balls are filled with toothsome ingredients like natural nut and seed butters, fiber-rich popcorn, rice crisp cereal, and buckwheat groats, as well as antioxidant-rich dried fruits and jelly and nutrient-loaded molasses. These components help satisfy your appetite and provide energy to last through the afternoon. They also work together to help ward off afternoon energy crashes and sugar cravings.

Active Ingredients

Brown Rice Crisp Cereal (Puffed Brown Rice)

This tasty, crunchy, and airy puffed grain is made from the world's second largest crop—rice. Brown rice is the whole rice kernel, which is loaded with fiber, copper, manganese, iron, and B vitamins. When added to energy balls, puffed brown rice adds crunch, flavor, and lightness, as well as providing energy that lasts for hours after lunch.

Buckwheat Groats

Buckwheat groats are the hulled seeds of the buckwheat plant. They are naturally gluten free, full of nutrients—including magnesium, manganese, copper, phosphorus, and B vitamins—and very rich in dietary fiber. They also contain protein, including all of the essential amino acids. In energy balls, buckwheat groats create bulk and add a nice crunchy texture. They also make the balls more filling and provide a slow-releasing, sustainable energy from the carbohydrates and fiber to get you through the afternoon without any postlunch sugar cravings.

Buckwheat groats

Figs

Figs are light, delicate, slightly sweet, and have a soft and chewy texture with little hints of crunch from the seeds. Both fresh and dried figs are rich in manganese, copper, calcium, magnesium, potassium, and vitamin K. They are also a source of dietary fiber, which helps fill you up. In energy balls, fresh figs add moisture, while dried figs add a sticky, chewy consistency and sweet flavor, and work as a binder for the other ingredients. There are many varieties of figs, but for the energy balls in this book, I use either ripe fresh figs or dried Black Mission and Turkish figs.

Natural Fruit Jelly or Jam

A peanut butter and jelly sandwich is a real lunch-box classic, and jelly can be a nice nutritional boost when it's the right kind. Fruit jams and jellies are typically made by boiling fruit or concentrated fruit juice with water and a sweetener until thickened. Choose a jam or jelly that has been naturally sweetened with fruit juice or unrefined sugars, such as cane sugar or coconut palm sugar. Because fruit is naturally high in nutrients, fruit jams and jellies contain vitamin C and provide energy through the natural fruit sugars. Natural fruit jelly is a great source of antioxidants, which are known to boost energy, so fruity lunchtime energy balls can be the perfect afternoon pick-me-up.

Popcorn

The kernels that popcorn is made from contain fiber, manganese, magnesium, and vitamin B_3, which makes it filling and tasty. Popcorn creates bulk and adds a light texture to energy balls. The healthiest popcorn is air-popped; you can pop it yourself and season lightly with salt, or toss in melted coconut oil or vegan butter. If you buy it prepared, look for air-popped popcorn that is plain or has only added salt and oil. Choose organic, non-GMO kernels or popcorn.

Popcorn

Strawberries

Strawberries are so full of vitamin C that just ¾ cup (105 g) of fresh fruit contains 97 percent of the daily recommended intake. Dried strawberries are dried in a dehydrator or oven, whereas freeze-dried strawberries are frozen followed by a vacuum-drying process. Because the fruit is not heated, the nutrients lost in the freeze-drying process are minimal. Thanks to the dietary fiber they contain, they are filling, and their natural sugars release more slowly than the refined sugar found in processed fruit snacks.

Sunflower-Seed Butter

Sunflower-seed butter is loaded with minerals, including copper, iron, manganese, magnesium, phosphorus, and zinc. It is also rich in B vitamins and healthy fats that support your nervous system and overall health. The butter adds a smooth, creamy richness to energy balls, and both moisture and a binding quality. Look for a butter with no additives or an unrefined sweetener such as cane sugar. While I generally recommend unsweetened nut and seed butters, sunflower-seed butter with a small amount of added cane sugar typically has a better flavor. It is also a great source of healthy fats, which are filling and stabilize blood sugar levels.

Unsulfured Molasses

A thick, sticky, bittersweet syrup, unsulfured molasses is made from sugarcane but is quite low in sugar, as it is what is leftover after the sugar has been boiled several times. It is full of vitamins and minerals, including magnesium, manganese, potassium, iron, calcium, and vitamin B_6, which makes it a great lunchtime ingredient. Buy "unsulfured" molasses to ensure it is free of sulfur dioxide, a common preservative. Blackstrap molasses contains more vitamins and minerals than other molasses and is the best choice. It is rich in iron, essential for energy production.

Molasses

Gingerbread– Dark Chocolate

MAKES 10 BALLS

¾ cup [120 g] pitted dates

1 cup [100 g] shredded unsweetened coconut

¼ cup [40 g] raw buckwheat groats

2 Tbsp chia seeds

2 Tbsp hemp seeds

1 tsp molasses

1 tsp ground cinnamon

½ tsp ground ginger

¼ tsp ground nutmeg

⅛ tsp ground cloves

FOR THE COATING

¼ cup [45 g] chopped dark chocolate

½ tsp coconut palm sugar

½ tsp ground ginger

SERVING SIZE: 1 BALL	
Calories	167
Protein	3 g
Fat	9 g
Carbohydrate	21 g
Sugar	12 g
Dietary fiber	4 g
Vitamins	B_6, B_3
Minerals	calcium, iron, potassium

Although gingerbread is a traditional holiday season treat, there's no reason why you can't enjoy this classic dessert all year round! The healthful fats in the coconut, chia, and hemp seeds combine with carbohydrates from the buckwheat, mineral-rich molasses, and all of the classic gingerbread spices to make a great healthy, energy-enhancing dessert. Added to that, these balls are nut-free.

1 Put the dates in a small heatproof bowl and cover them with hot water. Set aside for 10 to 15 minutes, until softened. Drain, reserving 2 Tbsp of the liquid and discarding the remainder.

2 In a food processor, combine the dates, the 2 Tbsp reserved soaking liquid, the coconut, buckwheat groats, chia and hemp seeds, molasses, and all of the spices and process for 1 to 2 minutes, until a sticky mass forms.

3 Using a tablespoon, scoop out a 2-Tbsp portion of the mixture and, with clean slightly wet hands, roll the mixture into a ball between your palms. Set the ball on a plate. Repeat with the remaining mixture until you have 10 balls slightly smaller than a golf ball. Place the balls in the freezer to set for 30 minutes.

4 Meanwhile, make the coating. Place the chocolate in a heatproof bowl set over a pan of simmering water, and stir until melted. Remove from the heat. Remove the balls from the freezer, pour 1 tsp of melted chocolate over each one, and sprinkle with the coconut palm sugar and ground ginger. Return to the freezer for another 30 minutes. Store in an airtight container in the freezer or refrigerator until required. Defrost as necessary before serving.

Try this!

Gingerbread and Lemon

Omit the chocolate coating. Add 1 Tbsp finely grated lemon zest and 1 Tbsp lemon juice to the food processor with the ingredients.

Gingerbread, Chia, and Chocolate Chip

Omit the hemp seeds and chocolate coating and increase the chia seeds to ¼ cup [40 g]; fold ⅓ cup [60 g] dark chocolate chips into the mixture before rolling it into balls.

For a deep chocolate hit, use a dark chocolate containing 70% cocoa solids to coat these balls.

Cocoa Crispy Rice

Many people love crispy rice squares, but they contain refined sugars that often cause blood sugar spikes and—eventually—energy crashes. These cereal balls bring the same chocolaty, chewy, and crunchy consistency, without the sugar high. The slow-release carbohydrates in the cereal, combined with the coconut palm sugar and brown rice syrup, mineral-dense cocoa powder, omega-rich almond butter, and shredded coconut, will keep you feeling full and satisfy your sweet tooth, as well.

1 In a large bowl, combine the crispy brown rice cereal, shredded coconut, coconut palm sugar, and cocoa powder and stir to combine.

2 Add the brown rice syrup and almond butter. Stir until well combined and a sticky mass forms.

3 Using a tablespoon, scoop the mixture and, with clean slightly wet hands, shape the mixture into a ball between your palms. Set the ball on a plate. Repeat with the remaining mixture until you have 10 golf ball–size balls.

4 Place the balls in the freezer to set for 1 hour. Store in an airtight container in the refrigerator until required; avoid exposure to warm temperatures or the balls will melt.

Try this!
Nut-Free Cocoa Crispy Rice Cereal
Omit the natural almond butter and replace with ⅓ cup [85 g] natural sunflower butter for a nut-free version that is safe to send to school with the kids.

MAKES 10 BALLS

1½ cups [40 g] crispy brown rice cereal

2 Tbsp shredded unsweetened coconut

1 Tbsp coconut palm sugar

1 Tbsp plain cocoa powder

6 Tbsp [110 g] brown rice syrup

6 Tbsp [100 g] natural almond butter

SERVING SIZE: 1 BALL	
Calories	145
Protein	3 g
Fat	6 g
Carbohydrate	20 g
Sugar	2 g
Dietary fiber	1 g
Vitamins	All B's
Minerals	iron, magnesium, manganese, phosphorus, selenium

Oatmeal and Raisin Cookie

Chewy, hearty oatmeal cookies always hit the spot. These energy balls have all the flavor and texture of this beloved cookie, along with nutrients to improve your energy levels. The oats, brown rice syrup, dates, and raisins all deliver carbohydrates that increase stamina levels to ward off that afternoon slump, along with minerals including iron, magnesium, calcium, and zinc. Meanwhile, protein- and omega-rich almonds and almond butter help to stabilize blood sugars and add a delicious nutty flavor.

MAKES 16 BALLS

1½ cups [210 g] raw almonds

½ cup [50 g] gluten-free rolled oats, plus 2 Tbsp

½ cup [80 g] pitted dates

¼ cup [65 g] natural almond butter

2 Tbsp brown rice syrup

2 Tbsp unsweetened almond milk

½ tsp pure vanilla extract

pinch of salt

⅓ cup [45 g] dark raisins

1 In a food processor, pulse the whole almonds for 2 to 3 minutes, until they have the consistency of almond meal. Add the ½ cup [50 g] rolled oats and process until combined.

2 Add the dates, almond butter, brown rice syrup, almond milk, vanilla, and salt and process for 1 to 2 minutes, until a sticky mass forms. Transfer to a bowl and stir in the 2 Tbsp rolled oats and the raisins.

3 Using a tablespoon, scoop the mixture and, with clean slightly wet hands, shape the mixture into a ball between your palms, using firm pressure. Set the ball on a plate. Repeat with the remaining mixture until you have 16 balls.

4 Place the balls in the freezer to set for 30 minutes. Store in an airtight container in the refrigerator or at room temperature until required. Bring to room temperature before serving.

Try this!

Oatmeal–Chocolate Chunk Cookie
Oatmeal cookies with chunks of rich chocolate? Yes, please! Treat yourself to this delicious variation by omitting the raisins and substituting ⅓ cup [40 g] vegan dark chocolate chunks.

Cinnamon Oatmeal Cookie
Omit the raisins. Add 1 tsp ground cinnamon to the food processor with the remaining ingredients for a spicy-and-sweet, metabolism-boosting cinnamon kick!

SERVING SIZE: 1 BALL	
Calories	161
Protein	4 g
Fat	9 g
Carbohydrate	18 g
Sugar	9 g
Dietary fiber	3 g
Vitamins	A, all B's, E
Minerals	calcium, iron, magnesium, zinc

Strawberry Shortcake

Most of us need no excuse to snack on a slice of cake at any time of day. While cake may not be healthy, these cake-flavored balls sure are! The fiber-rich coconut flour brings a lovely cake crumb to these balls, and dietary fiber from the flour keeps blood sugars stable. The combination of dried and freeze-dried strawberries add immune-strengthening vitamins C and E. The dried strawberries are soft and chewy, contrasting nicely with the crunchy, freeze-dried fruits.

MAKES 18 BALLS

1½ cups [210 g] raw almonds

½ cup [50 g] coconut flour

⅔ cup [16 g] freeze-dried strawberries (soaked for 10 minutes in hot water, then drained)

½ cup [12 g] dried strawberries

6 Tbsp [40 g] shredded unsweetened coconut

4 Tbsp [60 ml] full-fat coconut cream

2 Tbsp unsweetened almond milk

¼ tsp pure vanilla extract

1 In a food processor, pulse the almonds for 1 to 2 minutes, until they have the consistency of almond meal. Add the coconut flour and process until combined.

2 Add the freeze-dried and dried strawberries, shredded coconut, coconut cream, almond milk, and vanilla and process for 1 to 2 minutes, until a sticky mass forms.

3 Using a tablespoon, scoop the mixture and, with clean slightly wet hands, shape the mixture into a ball between your palms. Set the ball on a plate. Repeat with the remaining mixture until you have 18 balls.

4 Place the balls in the freezer to set for 30 minutes. Store in an airtight container in the refrigerator or at room temperature until required.

Try this!

Banana–Strawberry Shortcake
Add ½ cup [45 g] chopped freeze-dried bananas to the food processor with the other ingredients. The bananas give a fix of potassium to keep you going for the rest of the day!

SERVING SIZE: 1 BALL	
Calories	110
Protein	3 g
Fat	7 g
Carbohydrate	9 g
Sugar	5 g
Dietary fiber	3 g
Vitamins	B$_2$, C, E
Minerals	calcium, iron, magnesium, manganese

Peanut Butter and Jelly

Peanut butter and jelly were probably one of your go-to lunches as a kid; why change a good thing? These balls re-create that classic combo by using raw peanuts and peanut butter, which are both rich in magnesium and vitamin B_6 to enhance your mood, combined with naturally sweetened fruit jelly. The oats add bulk as they are rich in fiber; they are also high in complex carbohydrates to provide energy, not to mention B vitamins.

MAKES 14 BALLS

1¾ cups [280 g] pitted dates

½ cup [50 g] gluten-free quick oats

⅓ cup [45 g] raw peanuts

¼ cup [65 g] natural peanut butter

1 heaping Tbsp naturally sweetened fruit jelly

1 Combine the dates, oats, peanuts, and peanut butter in a food processor and process for 1 to 2 minutes, until combined. Pour in 3 Tbsp warm water and process for 1 to 2 minutes, until a sticky mass forms.

2 Using a tablespoon, scoop the mixture and, with clean slightly wet hands, shape the mixture into a ball between your palms. Create a deep well in the ball with a finger and spoon a scant ¼ tsp of fruit jelly into the well. Fold the ball around the well to seal and gently shape back into a ball. Set the ball on a plate. Repeat with the remaining mixture until you have 14 balls slightly smaller than a golf ball.

3 Place the balls in the freezer to set for 30 minutes. Store in an airtight container in the refrigerator until required, as they soften at room temperature.

Try this!
Cashew Butter and Jelly

Give this classic pairing a modern twist, using omega-rich cashews and cashew butter. Omit the peanuts and peanut butter and replace with ¼ cup [65 g] natural cashew butter and ⅓ cup [45 g] raw cashews.

SERVING SIZE: 1 BALL	
Calories	116
Protein	3 g
Fat	4 g
Carbohydrate	19 g
Sugar	12 g
Dietary fiber	3 g
Vitamins	all B's, C
Minerals	calcium, iron, magnesium

Sweet-and-Salty Popcorn

Popcorn is loaded with fiber and provides magnesium, iron, and even some protein. These balls combine the much-loved flavor of freshly popped corn with sweet dates and brown rice syrup; silky sunflower-seed butter; fiber-rich flaxseed; and just the right amount of sea salt. It's the perfect snack when you crave something sweet and salty, and the energy from these balls will help to sustain you through the afternoon. Popcorn doesn't have to be just for the movies!

MAKES 10 BALLS

1 cup [160 g] pitted dates

¼ cup [65 g] sunflower-seed butter (unsweetened or sweetened with cane sugar)

2 Tbsp brown rice syrup

2 Tbsp ground flaxseed

½ tsp pure vanilla extract

¼ tsp sea salt

6 cups [48 g] freshly popped and cooled popcorn

2 Tbsp unsweetened coconut milk from a carton

1 Combine the dates, sunflower-seed butter, brown rice syrup, flaxseed, vanilla, and sea salt in a food processor and process on low for 30 seconds. Scrape down the sides of the bowl, then process on high for about 30 seconds, until a crumbly mass forms.

2 Add 4 cups [32 g] of the popcorn and process on low. Slowly pour in the coconut milk and process for 15 to 30 seconds, until a sticky mass starts to form. Transfer to a large mixing bowl.

3 Wash and dry the food processor. Place the remaining 2 cups [16 g] of the popcorn in the work bowl of the food processor and process on high for 10 to 30 seconds, until it is broken into small pieces. Spread the popcorn pieces on a plate.

4 Using a tablespoon, scoop the date mixture and, with clean slightly wet hands, roll and lightly squeeze the mixture into a ball between your palms. Roll in the popcorn pieces to lightly coat, and set on a separate plate. Repeat with the remaining mixture until you have 10 balls, each just smaller than a golf ball.

5 Place the balls in the freezer to set for 30 minutes. Store in an airtight container in the refrigerator until required.

Try this!

Almond Butter, Dark Chocolate, and Popcorn

Use nuts and 70 percent cacao solids vegan dark chocolate for a grown-up treat. Replace the ¼ cup [65 g] sunflower-seed butter with ¼ cup [65 g] natural almond butter and add 2 Tbsp chopped chocolate to the food processor with the popcorn.

SERVING SIZE: 1 BALL	
Calories	134
Protein	2 g
Fat	4 g
Carbohydrate	22 g
Sugar	13 g
Dietary fiber	3 g
Vitamins	B$_6$
Minerals	copper, iron, magnesium, manganese, potassium

To save time—and add flavor—use a natural pre-popped bagged popcorn flavored with olive oil and sea salt.

Fig and Almond

MAKES 14 BALLS

4 fresh figs
[200 g]

1 cup [160 g] dried
black Mission figs

½ cup [80 g] dried
Turkish figs

½ cup [70 g] raw almonds

1 Tbsp finely grated
orange zest

1 Tbsp fresh orange juice

1¼ tsp ground cinnamon

½ tsp pure vanilla extract

1½ Tbsp almond flour or meal
or ground almonds

1½ Tbsp gluten-free oat bran

1½ Tbsp coconut palm sugar

SERVING SIZE: 1 BALL	
Calories	102
Protein	2 g
Fat	3 g
Carbohydrate	19 g
Sugar	13 g
Dietary fiber	4 g
Vitamins	B_2, C, E, K
Minerals	copper, magnesium, manganese, phosphorus, potassium

Fig rolls and cookies have long added a bit of fiber to the nation's lunch boxes. This recipe transforms the classic confection by using whole-food ingredients and unrefined sugars to make a perfect midday pick-me-up! The filling combines fresh and dried figs to provide energy as well as vitamin K, potassium, and manganese. There are additional nutrients in the orange juice, plus flavor from the cinnamon, vanilla, and almonds. Instead of a pastry shell, the fruit filling is rolled in a healthy coating of almond flour, fiber-rich oat bran, coconut palm sugar, and more cinnamon.

1 Combine the fresh, black Mission, and Turkish figs; almonds; orange zest and juice; ½ tsp of the cinnamon; and the vanilla in a food processor and process on low for 15 seconds. Scrape down the sides of the bowl with a spatula and process for 10 seconds. Repeat until the ingredients are combined and a sticky mass forms. Transfer to a large bowl and place in the freezer while you prepare the coating.

2 Combine the almond flour, oat bran, coconut palm sugar, and remaining ¾ tsp cinnamon in a small bowl.

3 Remove the fig mixture from the freezer. Using a tablespoon, scoop the mixture and, with clean slightly wet hands, shape the mixture into a ball between your palms, roll in the almond-flour mixture to lightly coat, and set on a plate. Repeat with the remaining mixture until you have 14 balls, each just smaller than a golf ball.

4 Place the balls in the freezer to set for 30 minutes. Store in an airtight container in the refrigerator until required.

Try this!
Cherries and Figs
Bring the antioxidant, immune-boosting power and sweet, tart flavor of dried cherries to these balls. Reduce the dried black Mission figs to ½ cup [80 g] and add ½ cup [60 g] dried unsweetened cherries.

Peanut Butter and Chocolate

Peanut butter and chocolate are a dream duo, so it's no wonder that the peanut butter cup remains a favorite. Here's how to enjoy the flavors of this delicious treat without the not-so-healthy ingredients. This recipe combines the good fats found in raw peanuts and almonds with the natural sweetness of dates, antioxidant rich dark chocolate, iron-rich cocoa powder, sea salt, and almond milk. The balls are coated in a creamy, peanut butter shell. The perfect nutritious sweet for any lunch box!

MAKES 12 BALLS

1 cup [160 g] pitted dates

1 cup [140 g] raw peanuts, plus 2 Tbsp crushed

½ cup [70 g] raw almonds

2 Tbsp chopped 70% cacao solids vegan dark chocolate, plus 2 Tbsp shavings

2 Tbsp plain cocoa powder

pinch of sea salt

¼ cup [60 ml] unsweetened almond milk

FOR THE COATING

2 Tbsp coconut oil

¼ cup [65 g] natural peanut butter

1 Combine the dates, whole peanuts, almonds, chopped chocolate, cocoa, and sea salt in a food processor and process on low for 30 seconds, then on high for 30 seconds. Reduce the speed to low, pour in the almond milk, and process until a sticky mass forms.

2 Using a tablespoon, scoop the mixture and, with clean slightly wet hands, shape the mixture into a ball between your palms, and set on a plate. Repeat with the remaining mixture until you have 12 balls, each just smaller than a golf ball.

3 Place the balls in the freezer to set for 30 minutes. After about 20 minutes, make the coating. Melt the coconut oil in a saucepan over low heat. Add the peanut butter and stir constantly until smooth. Remove from the heat and transfer to a bowl.

4 Place one of the frozen balls on the tip of a skewer or toothpick. Dip into the coating, lift it out, and rotate until set (but not hard). Remove the ball from the skewer without touching the coating and put it on a separate plate. Repeat with the remaining balls, then sprinkle them with the crushed peanuts and chocolate shavings.

5 Return the balls to the freezer for 30 minutes. Store in an airtight container in the refrigerator and serve chilled.

Try this!

Peanut Butter and Cacao Nibs

Add the antioxidant power of cacao nibs to these balls. Replace the 2 Tbsp chopped vegan dark chocolate with 1 heaping Tbsp natural raw cacao nibs and add 2 Tbsp natural peanut butter with the other ingredients. Do not coat the balls.

SERVING SIZE: 1 BALL	
Calories	203
Protein	6 g
Fat	14 g
Carbohydrate	16 g
Sugar	10 g
Dietary fiber	3 g
Vitamins	B_2, B_6, E
Minerals	copper, iron, magnesium, manganese

For a quick coating, simply drizzle the balls with the peanut butter mixture.

Apricot, Coconut, and Seeds

MAKES 14 BALLS

1½ cups [270 g] dried apricots

½ cup [50 g] shredded unsweetened coconut

¼ cup [65 g] unsweetened sunflower-seed butter

1 tsp coconut palm sugar

pinch of salt

2 heaping Tbsp raw sesame seeds

2 heaping Tbsp raw poppy seeds

2 heaping Tbsp raw hemp seeds

2 heaping Tbsp raw pumpkin seeds

2 heaping Tbsp raw sunflower seeds

2 Tbsp unsweetened coconut milk

SERVING SIZE: 1 BALL	
Calories	131
Protein	3 g
Fat	7 g
Carbohydrate	14 g
Sugar	7 g
Dietary fiber	3 g
Vitamins	A, B_6, E
Minerals	calcium, magnesium, manganese, potassium, selenium

If you're searching for a healthy, nut-free snack, then these seed-packed balls are what you're looking for! They combine sweet, vitamin C–packed apricots with magnesium from the coconut, and healthy fats, protein, vitamins, and minerals from the raw pumpkin, poppy, sesame, hemp, and sunflower seeds. The seeds also provide a little crunch to balance out the chewy texture of the antioxidant rich apricots and smooth richness of the sunflower-seed butter.

1 Combine the apricots, coconut, sunflower-seed butter, coconut palm sugar, and salt in a food processor and process for 1 to 2 minutes, until well combined and a crumbly mass forms. Add the sesame, poppy, hemp, pumpkin, and sunflower seeds and process on low speed. Pour in the coconut milk and process for 1 to 2 minutes, until a sticky mass starts to come together.

2 Using a tablespoon, scoop the mixture and, with clean slightly wet hands, shape the mixture into a ball between your palms, squeezing it if necessary, and set on a plate. Repeat with the remaining mixture until you have 14 balls, each just smaller than a golf ball.

3 Place the balls in the refrigerator to set for 30 minutes. Store in an airtight container in the refrigerator or at room temperature until required.

Try this!
Apricot, Banana, and Seeds
Apricot and banana is a surprising flavor combination that really works. Both fruits are sweet and equally healthy—plus, the banana brings potassium to these energy balls. Reduce the dried apricots to 1 cup [180 g] and add ½ cup [45 g] chopped dehydrated banana (not banana chips).

If your sunflower seed butter is already sweetened, omit the 1 tsp coconut palm sugar.

[Brain-Boosting

Energy Balls]

Feel empowered to take on whatever the day brings
with these tasty, easy-to-make recipes filled with
brain food! All of the balls in this chapter contain
healthy ingredients like omega-filled nuts and
avocado, antioxidant-rich fruits, superfoods such
as spirulina powder, and natural caffeine sources
like matcha and chai. These whole-food ingredients
provide nutrients that are known to enhance
concentration, increase focus, and support the
mental stamina required for work and study.

Brain-Boosting Energy Balls
Active Ingredients

Avocado

Avocado

This rich, creamy fruit is known for its healthy unsaturated fats rich in omega-3s. These are essential for brain and nervous system health and have been linked to improved memory, mood, and cognitive function. In energy balls, the flavorful flesh adds a creamy, rich consistency and a bit of moisture. While avocados are generally subtle in taste, they create a rich chocolate pudding flavor when combined with a natural sweetener and cocoa powder.

Bananas (Whole Natural Dried)

When people think of dried bananas, they often think of the usual banana chips, which are used in small doses in this book. Naturally dried bananas contain no added oils or sweeteners, although some may have been treated with lime or lemon juice or citric acid. They are soft and chewy, and rich in potassium and vitamin B_6, which are important for the nervous system and brain health and boost cognitive function. Be sure to look for unsulfured varieties.

Brazil Nuts

Brazil nuts are rich in nutrients, including magnesium and selenium. Selenium has a huge impact on brain function; it is an essential nutrient for nerve cells, as it promotes the production of glutathione, one of the brain's most beneficial antioxidants. These powerhouse nuts also add crunch and bulk to energy balls.

Coffee

The caffeine found in ground coffee beans has been shown to improve memory, mental performance, alertness, attention, and concentration. While I don't recommend drinking several cups of coffee per day (especially as that often brings with it sugar, milk, or cream), I do think that a small dose of ground coffee in an energy ball can boost the brain, and the body will benefit from the nutritional attributes of the ingredients. I recommend organic, fair-trade ground coffee, which is better for both the body and the environment.

Dried Super Fruits

You can choose any combination of fruits and berries in the recipes calling for dried fruit, but I recommend dried unsweetened cherries, blueberries, cranberries, goji berries, and golden berries. All of these fruits are loaded with vitamin C (a powerful antioxidant) and fiber. If you use a premixed bag sold as an "antioxidant mix," the combination of fruits should provide an ample amount of antioxidants, which may help to combat aging as well as enhance memory and overall cognitive function.

Masala Chai Tea Powder

This is a combination of black tea leaves; spices such as cinnamon, ginger, cloves, cardamom, and pepper; and a natural sweetener such as cane sugar, that have been ground together into a powder. The caffeine from the tea boosts alertness and mental function, and the vitamins and minerals in the spices are delivered as well.

Matcha

This bright green powder is made by grinding the leaves of a Japanese green tea that contains a hundred times more antioxidants than regular brewed green tea. It also brings L-theanine, an amino acid that aids mental clarity and concentration. In energy balls, matcha adds a slightly bitter flavor that on its own could be overpowering, but when combined with sweet dates and chocolate, it has a great flavor.

Matcha

Spirulina Powder

Spirulina is a freshwater algae that can be consumed by humans. To make the powder, the algae is dried using a technique that preserves the carotenes and fatty acids it contains, and then ground. Spirulina also contains calcium, iron, potassium, magnesium, and B vitamins. Studies have shown that even a small dose can boost academic performance. The powder adds a deep green hue and a mild earthy flavor to energy balls, and is especially delicious when combined with sweet dates and other ingredients.

Walnuts

Walnuts are rich in omega-3 fatty acids known to boost brain and cognitive function. They may also help prevent neurological conditions such as Alzheimer's disease. The raw nuts contain B vitamins, which support nervous system health. In energy balls, these nuts provide moisture, bulk, crunch, and a soft, mild nutty flavor.

Walnuts

Hazelnut-Super Fruit

You could say that these balls are "beauty food" for the brain. Hazelnuts are laden with magnesium and vitamin B_6, which support brain function and mental clarity. The dried berries add antioxidants that help prevent inflammation in the brain and to slow down the aging process. The nuts and fruits, with the healthful fats from the almonds and power-giving carbohydrates from the dates and oats, make for a great snack.

MAKES 14 BALLS

¾ cup [120 g] pitted dates

¾ cup [90 g] dried berry mixture

½ cup [70 g] raw almonds

½ cup [60 g] raw hazelnuts

¼ cup [25 g] gluten-free rolled oats

2 Tbsp unsweetened almond milk, plus 1 Tbsp (optional)

1 tsp pure vanilla extract

1 In a food processor, combine the dates, berry mix, almonds, hazelnuts, oats, the 2 Tbsp almond milk, and the vanilla and process for 2 minutes, until well incorporated. Leave larger chunks of nuts and berries in the mass, or process to a smoother consistency by adding the 1 Tbsp almond milk, if desired.

2 Using a tablespoon, scoop the mixture and, with clean slightly wet hands, shape the mixture into a ball between your palms. Set the ball on a plate. Repeat with the remaining mixture until you have 14 balls slightly smaller than a golf ball.

3 Place the balls in the freezer to set for 30 minutes. Store in an airtight container in the refrigerator or at room temperature until required.

Try this!

Vanilla Protein-Super Fruit

Up your protein intake and the vanilla flavor of these delicious balls by omitting the ¼ cup [25 g] oats and replacing them with ¼ cup [30 g] vanilla vegan protein powder.

Hazelnut-Golden Berry

Omit the ¾ cup [90 g] dried berry mixture and add ¾ cup [90 g] golden berries, a Peruvian superfood. The tart yellow berries taste great with the hazelnuts and bring even more antioxidants.

SERVING SIZE: 1 BALL	
Calories	112
Protein	5 g
Fat	6 g
Carbohydrate	11 g
Sugar	8 g
Dietary fiber	2 g
Vitamins	A, all B's, C
Minerals	calcium, iron, magnesium

If you cannot
find mixed dried
berries you can make
your own by mixing three or
four different fruits, such as
dried blueberries, cherries,
cranberries, golden berries,
or strawberries.

Chocolate Chip and Banana

Ever since the first banana split was made, chocolate and banana have been a dynamic duo. These energy balls take it up a level with the addition of raw walnuts. Both walnuts and bananas are packed with vitamin B_6, which helps to keep the nervous system healthy and enhances serotonin production to maintain positive thoughts. The dried whole bananas have a soft and chewy consistency, while the banana chips add crunch. Looking for a mood and brain boost? Put these balls at the top of the list.

1 In a food processor, combine the chopped dried bananas, dates, cashews, walnuts, banana chips, and coconut flour and process for 30 seconds to 1 minute, until well combined.

2 Pour in the almond milk and process again for about 30 seconds, until a sticky and crumbly mass forms. Transfer to a large bowl and fold in the dark chocolate chips.

3 Using a tablespoon, scoop the mixture and, with clean slightly wet hands, shape the mixture into a ball between your palms. The mixture will feel "wet" to the touch. Wrap the ball in a piece of paper towel or cheesecloth and squeeze to extract excess moisture and bind the ingredients so that the ball maintains its shape. Set the ball on a plate. Repeat with the remaining mixture until you have 10 golf ball–size balls.

4 Place the balls in the freezer to set for 30 minutes. Store in an airtight container in the refrigerator until required. Serve chilled or at room temperature.

Try this!
Chocolate Chip, Carob, and Banana
Are you a carob fan? Then you'll love this easy substitution. Reduce the coconut flour to 1 Tbsp and add 1 Tbsp raw carob powder, which will lend a richer flavor to the balls and adds calcium and vitamin B_2—both awesome brain-enhancing nutrients.

MAKES 10 BALLS

1 cup [100 g] chopped whole dried bananas

½ cup [80 g] pitted dates

½ cup [70 g] raw cashews

½ cup [60 g] raw walnut halves

½ cup [50 g] banana chips

2 Tbsp coconut flour

2 Tbsp unsweetened almond milk

2 heaping Tbsp mini vegan dark chocolate chips

SERVING SIZE: 1 BALL	
Calories	138
Protein	3 g
Fat	7 g
Carbohydrate	16 g
Sugar	10 g
Dietary fiber	2 g
Vitamins	B_6
Minerals	iron, magnesium, potassium

Lemon and Brazil Nut

Lemons, raw Brazil nuts, oats, dates, and coconut nectar come together in these sweet-yet-tart balls. Lemons are a fantastic source of vitamins, notably vitamin C, which supports healthy brain function. It is also an antioxidant and helps to prevent free-radical damage in the brain. The Brazil nuts provide selenium, a mineral that preserves brain health and promotes cognitive function, giving you sharp mental clarity.

MAKES 15 BALLS

1 cup [160 g] pitted dates

1 cup [125 g] raw Brazil nuts

¼ cup [25 g] gluten-free rolled oats

1 Tbsp fresh lemon juice, plus 2 Tbsp finely grated zest

1 Tbsp coconut or agave nectar

⅛ tsp pure lemon extract

1 tsp ground cinnamon

1 In a food processor, combine the dates, Brazil nuts, oats, lemon juice, 1 Tbsp of the lemon zest, the coconut nectar, and the lemon extract and process for 1 to 2 minutes, until a sticky mass forms.

2 Spread the remaining 1 Tbsp lemon zest on a plate. Using a tablespoon, scoop the mixture and, with clean slightly wet hands, shape the mixture into a ball between your palms. The mixture will feel "wet" to the touch. Wrap the ball in a piece of paper towel or cheesecloth and squeeze to extract excess moisture and bind the ingredients so that the ball maintains its shape.

3 Roll the ball in the lemon zest to lightly coat, and set on a plate. Sprinkle the top of the ball with a pinch of ground cinnamon. Repeat with the remaining mixture until you have 15 balls, each just smaller than a golf ball.

4 Place the balls in the freezer to set for 30 minutes. Store in an airtight container in the refrigerator or at room temperature until required.

SERVING SIZE: 1 BALL	
Calories	138
Protein	3 g
Fat	8 g
Carbohydrate	15 g
Sugar	9 g
Dietary fiber	2 g
Vitamins	all B's, C
Minerals	calcium, magnesium, selenium

Try this!

Orange and Brazil Nut

Exchange the lemon for another fruit bursting with vitamin C—an orange. Omit the lemon juice, zest, and extract and add 1 Tbsp fresh orange juice, plus 1 Tbsp finely grated zest and ⅛ tsp pure orange extract. Roll the balls in 1 Tbsp finely grated orange zest.

Lemon, Rosemary, and Brazil Nut

If you love a sweet-and-savory flavor combination, add ½ tsp dried rosemary to the mixture before processing.

Chocolate, Almond, and Sea Salt

A healthy brain thrives on nutritional balance. These balls achieve that with a fusion of complex carbohydrates from the oats (which are also rich in B vitamins to support the nervous system), omega-rich fats from the almonds, and blood sugar–stabilizing protein from the protein powder. "Brain fog" might mean that your blood sugars are out of whack; the protein in these balls will help maintain blood sugars and keep low brain power at bay. Sea salt combined with chocolate and almonds is both a taste treat and a way to add even more minerals.

MAKES 24 BALLS

1 cup [160 g] pitted dates

1 cup [140 g] raw almonds

1 cup [120 g] vegan chocolate protein powder

1 cup [100 g] gluten-free rolled oats

3 Tbsp plain cocoa powder

2 Tbsp dark chocolate chips

½ tsp sea salt

½ cup [120 ml] unsweetened almond milk

24 small raw almonds

1 In a food processor, combine the dates, almonds, protein powder, oats, cocoa powder, chocolate chips, and ¼ tsp of the sea salt and process on high for 1 minute.

2 Reduce the speed to low, pour the almond milk through the top opening, and continue processing the mixture for 1 to 2 minutes, until a sticky mass forms.

3 Using a tablespoon, scoop the mixture and, with clean slightly wet hands, shape the mixture into a ball between your palms, and set on a plate. Press a small almond into the top of the ball and sprinkle with a pinch of sea salt. Repeat with the remaining mixture until you have 24 balls, each just smaller than a golf ball.

4 Place the balls in the freezer to set for 30 minutes. Store in an airtight container in the refrigerator until required. Serve slightly chilled or at room temperature.

Try this!
Vanilla, Almond, and Cinnamon
Exchange the chocolate and sea salt flavors of the balls for vanilla and a touch of cinnamon. Replace the chocolate protein powder with 1 cup [120 g] vegan vanilla protein powder, omit the cocoa powder, and replace the sea salt with 1 tsp ground cinnamon. Add ½ tsp of the cinnamon to the mixture in the food processor and sprinkle the remaining ½ tsp over the balls as a garnish.

SERVING SIZE: 1 BALL	
Calories	108
Protein	6 g
Fat	5 g
Carbohydrate	12 g
Sugar	5 g
Dietary fiber	3 g
Vitamins	all B's, E
Minerals	calcium, iron, magnesium, manganese

Mocha-Walnut

Can't go a day without your cup of joe? These balls, made with walnuts, almond meal, cocoa powder, ground coffee, coconut nectar, almond milk, and dates, will give you the same mental energy hit that you get from your daily coffee. Along with a little caffeine to stimulate your mental function, they are loaded with other brain-boosting nutrients, such as B vitamins from the walnuts, almonds, and dates. B vitamins are also known to support the nervous system and to help to put you in a good mood.

MAKES 14 BALLS

1 cup [120 g] walnut halves

½ cup [60 g] almond meal or flour or ground almonds

2 Tbsp plain cocoa powder

1 Tbsp ground coffee beans

1 cup [160 g] pitted dates

1 Tbsp coconut nectar

pinch of salt

1 Tbsp almond milk

1 Combine the walnuts, almond meal, cocoa powder, and ground coffee beans in a food processor and process until crumbly. Add the dates, coconut nectar, and salt and process for about 1 minute, until combined. Pour in the almond milk and process again until a sticky and crumbly mass forms.

2 Using a tablespoon, scoop the mixture and, with clean slightly wet hands, shape the mixture into a ball between your palms, squeezing it if necessary, and set on a plate. If the mixture appears oily, wrap the ball in a paper towel to absorb the excess moisture. Repeat with the remaining mixture until you have 14 balls, each just smaller than a golf ball.

3 Place the balls in the refrigerator to set for 30 minutes. Store in an airtight container in the refrigerator until required.

Try this!
Coffee and Walnut
If you really want the coffee flavor to dominate, omit the 2 Tbsp cocoa powder and use an additional 2 Tbsp almond meal.

SERVING SIZE: 1 BALL	
Calories	111
Protein	3 g
Fat	7 g
Carbohydrate	13 g
Sugar	9 g
Dietary fiber	2 g
Vitamins	B_1, B_2, B_6, E, folic acid
Minerals	copper, iron, magnesium, manganese, phosphorus, potassium

Matcha, Mint, and Chocolate

MAKES 12 BALLS

1 cup [140 g] raw cashews

10 pitted dates

½ cup [60 g] almond meal or flour or ground almonds, plus 1 tsp

2 Tbsp natural cocoa powder, plus ½ tsp

2 Tbsp coconut or agave nectar

½ tsp peppermint extract

1 Tbsp matcha

1 tsp finely chopped vegan dark chocolate

SERVING SIZE: 1 BALL	
Calories	131
Protein	4 g
Fat	7 g
Carbohydrate	13 g
Sugar	8 g
Dietary fiber	2 g
Vitamins	A, B_1, B_2, B_6, E, K
Minerals	copper, magnesium, manganese, phosphorus, potassium

If you're looking for a caffeine fix without coffee, then matcha (a green tea powder) is the way to go. Matcha is loaded with antioxidants and, while it contains caffeine to give your brain a boost, it also contains an amino acid called L-Theanine, which doesn't leave you with that wired feeling. With matcha, you'll experience mental clarity and motivation without the jitters. Plus these ingredients contain antioxidants that help to boost brain health, memory, and prevent damage that can occur in the brain though the aging process.

1 Put the cashews in a food processor and process until they form a crumbly meal. Add the dates, the ½ cup [60 g] almond meal, and the 2 Tbsp cocoa powder and process for 30 seconds. Add the coconut nectar, peppermint extract, and 2 Tbsp water and process until a sticky mass forms. Transfer the mixture to a large bowl.

2 In a small bowl, combine the matcha and the 1 tsp almond meal.

3 Using a tablespoon, scoop the mixture and, with clean slightly wet hands, shape the mixture into a ball between your palms, roll it in the almond and matcha mixture to lightly coat, then set on a plate. Repeat with the remaining mixture until you have 12 balls, each just smaller than a golf ball. Sprinkle the coated balls with the finely chopped vegan dark chocolate.

4 Place the balls in the refrigerator to set for 30 minutes. Store in an airtight container in the refrigerator or at room temperature until required.

Try this!

Matcha, Cashew, and Coconut

For a different flavor hit, combine the matcha with shredded coconut. Replace the peppermint extract and cocoa powder with ¼ cup [25 g] shredded unsweetened coconut and 1 Tbsp matcha. Omit the final sprinkle of chopped chocolate.

The almond meal
is an essential part of
the coating as without
it the matcha
would be absorbed
into the balls.

Vanilla Chai Latte

MAKES 14 BALLS

1 cup [160 g] pitted dates

½ cup [70 g] raw almonds

½ cup [50 g] coconut flour

3 Tbsp coconut butter

1 tsp chai tea powder

¼ tsp vanilla powder or pure vanilla extract

¼ cup [60 ml] unsweetened coconut milk from a carton

FOR THE COATING

2 Tbsp coconut butter

1 heaping Tbsp cocoa butter

½ Tbsp pure maple syrup

¼ tsp chai tea powder

1½ Tbsp unsweetened coconut milk from a carton

½ tsp coconut palm sugar

SERVING SIZE: 1 BALL	
Calories	164
Protein	4 g
Fat	11 g
Carbohydrate	16 g
Sugar	3 g
Dietary fiber	1 g
Vitamins	B_2, B_6, E
Minerals	copper, magnesium, manganese, potassium, selenium

Nothing is more comforting than a hot cup of tea, and when that tea is chai, it's a brain-booster, too. These balls combine chai tea with vanilla, energy-giving dates, healthy almonds, and filling coconut. The black tea in chai contains caffeine, which revs up mental function. Chai also contains spices such as cinnamon, which increase circulation and awareness while reducing fatigue. Plus, the ingredients in chai provide antioxidants, improve immune function, and reduce inflammation.

1 Combine the dates, almonds, coconut flour, coconut butter, chai tea powder, and vanilla in a food processor and process on low for 30 seconds, then on high for 30 seconds, until a crumbly mass forms. Return to low speed, pour in the coconut milk, and process for about 1 minute, until a sticky mass forms.

2 Using a tablespoon, scoop the mixture and, with clean slightly wet hands, shape the mixture into a ball between your palms, then set on a plate. Repeat with the remaining mixture until you have 14 balls, each just smaller than a golf ball. Place the balls in the freezer to set for 20 minutes.

3 Meanwhile, make the coating. Combine the coconut butter, cocoa butter, maple syrup, and chai tea powder in a saucepan and cook over low heat until melted and smooth. Transfer to a bowl and whisk in the coconut milk.

4 Remove the balls from the freezer and place one on the tip of a skewer or toothpick. Dip the ball into the coating mixture, lift it out, and rotate while the coating sets. (The color may look uneven at first but it will turn white as it hardens.) Remove the ball from the skewer and place on a clean plate. Repeat to cover all the balls, then sprinkle them with the coconut palm sugar.

5 Place the balls in the freezer to set for 30 minutes. Store in an airtight container in the refrigerator until required.

Try this!

Vanilla-Protein Chai Latte

Up the protein content by adding vanilla protein powder. Reduce the coconut flour to 2 Tbsp and add 2 Tbsp vegan vanilla protein powder with the rest of the ingredients. Omit the coating.

Chocolate, Almond, and Avocado

Avocado is the real star of this recipe, but you wouldn't know it from the taste! The flavor of the avocado is almost undetectable, but its creamy flesh creates a velvety, fudgelike texture and brings essential fatty-acid goodness. Essential fatty acids such as omega-3 are plentiful in avocado. These fats have been shown to improve mood and memory. The dates and maple syrup balance out the fats in these balls, bringing in some unrefined simple carbohydrates for an energy burst. Almonds add more healthy fats and some protein to boot.

MAKES 14 BALLS

1 cup [120 g] almond meal or flour or ground almonds, plus 2 Tbsp

½ cup [80 g] pitted dates

1 ripe avocado, pitted and peeled

¼ cup [20 g] plain cocoa powder, plus 1 Tbsp, plus ½ tsp

2 Tbsp pure maple syrup

pinch of salt

1 Combine the 1 cup [120 g] almond meal and the dates in a food processor and process until blended. Add the avocado, ¼ cup [20 g] cocoa powder, the maple syrup, and the salt and process for 1 to 2 minutes, until a sticky mass forms. Transfer the mixture to a large bowl and place in the freezer for 10 minutes.

2 Meanwhile, combine the 2 Tbsp almond meal and 1 Tbsp cocoa powder in a small bowl, then spread on a plate.

3 Remove the avocado mixture from the freezer. Using a tablespoon, scoop the mixture and, with clean slightly wet hands, shape the mixture into a ball between your palms, roll lightly in the almond meal and cocoa mixture to coat, then set on a plate. Repeat with the remaining mixture until you have 14 balls, each just smaller than a golf ball. Sprinkle the balls with the ½ tsp cocoa powder.

4 Place the balls in the freezer to set for 30 minutes. Store in an airtight container in the refrigerator until required, then serve slightly chilled or at room temperature.

Try this!
Chocolate, Pistachio, and Avocado

Pistachios are a fantastic source of vitamin B_6, known for its benefits when it comes to brain and mood support. By replacing the coating with ¼ cup [30 g] crushed pistachios, you'll get extra B_6 along with a yummy pistachio crunch.

SERVING SIZE: 1 BALL	
Calories	116
Protein	3 g
Fat	4 g
Carbohydrate	19 g
Sugar	12 g
Dietary fiber	3 g
Vitamins	all B's, C, E
Minerals	calcium, iron, magnesium

Spirulina and Hemp

Deep green and nutrient dense, spirulina is a superfood from the sea. This ocean algae is beneficial to cognitive function and overall health. It contains ample amounts of calcium, iron, potassium, magnesium, and B vitamins, and studies have shown that it can boost academic performance. The green powder pairs wonderfully with almonds, which contain healthy fats for brain function. Dates add energy, maple syrup brings natural sweetness, and hemp hearts contain more healthy fats and added protein. The spirulina flavor doesn't overpower the subtly sweet flavor of the balls.

1 Combine the dates, almonds, ¼ cup [30 g] of the hemp hearts, the spirulina, the maple syrup, and the salt in a food processor and process on high for 30 seconds. Pour in the almond milk and process on low for 30 seconds, until a sticky mass forms.

2 Spread the remaining ¼ cup [30 g] hulled hemp hearts on a large plate.

3 Using a tablespoon, scoop the mixture and, with clean slightly wet hands, shape the mixture into a ball between your palms, roll lightly in the hemp hearts to coat, and set on a plate. Repeat with the remaining mixture until you have 14 balls, each just smaller than a golf ball.

4 Place the balls in the freezer to set for 30 minutes. Store in an airtight container in the refrigerator or at room temperature until required.

Try this!

Spirulina and Sesame

For a different flavor—and the added benefits of calcium, magnesium, iron, and vitamin B—roll the balls in sesame seeds. Omit the ¼ cup [30 g] hulled hemp hearts for the coating and replace with ¼ cup [35 g] raw sesame seeds. For a stronger sesame flavor use toasted sesame seeds.

MAKES 14 BALLS

1 cup [160 g] pitted dates

1 cup [140 g] raw almonds

½ cup [60 g] hulled hemp hearts

1 Tbsp spirulina powder

2 tsp pure maple syrup

pinch of salt

1 Tbsp unsweetened almond milk

SERVING SIZE: 1 BALL	
Calories	137
Protein	5 g
Fat	8 g
Carbohydrate	12 g
Sugar	9 g
Dietary fiber	2 g
Vitamins	B_1, B_2, B_3, B_5, B_6, E
Minerals	calcium, copper, iron, magnesium, manganese, potassium

Performance-Enhancing
Energy Balls

These mouthwatering, simple, and delicious recipes are bursting with ingredients that take performance to the next level. They contain natural vegan protein powders, antioxidant-rich fruits and vegetables, protein-packed nut butters and hemp seeds, and energy-dense chickpeas. These ingredients all contain performance-specific nutrients that will help to increase strength and boost stamina, and are known to aid postexercise recovery.

Performance-Enhancing Energy Balls
Active Ingredients

Apricots

Dried apricots are simply apricots that have been halved, pitted, and dehydrated. Turkey is one of the world's top producers, hence the popularity of dried Turkish apricots. Apricots are loaded with antioxidants, including vitamin A, which boosts eye function. These golden fruits are rich in fiber and provide a wonderfully sweet, slightly tart, soft, and chewy addition to energy balls. Like dates, they are soft and sticky, so they also work well as a binding ingredient and lend a wonderful bright orange hue. Look for natural dried unsulfured apricots.

Carrots

Carrots are a fantastic source of vitamins A, B_6, C, and K and the minerals molybdenum and potassium. In fact, just half a raw carrot contains 100 percent of the daily recommended intake of vitamin A, a powerful antioxidant that increases eye function and reduces inflammation in the body. Carrots bring a beautiful orange color, a slightly sweet and earthy taste, and nutrients and dietary fiber to energy balls.

Cashew Butter

Creamy, smooth, nutty, and delicious, natural cashew butter is the new peanut butter, and really knocks it out of the park when it comes to nutritional content. It is rich in healthy unsaturated fats, protein, magnesium, vitamin B_6, and iron. Iron in particular is known to increase aerobic capacity, giving the body the ability to do more aerobic activity for a longer period of time. In energy balls, cashew butter adds moisture, binds ingredients, and provides a rich, creamy texture. Natural cashew butter is made from blended raw or roasted cashews—that's all.

Carrots

Chickpeas

Chickpeas, also known as garbanzo beans, are legumes that contain ample amounts of protein, and are a great complex carbohydrate for preworkout energy and performance enhancement. They also contain plenty of dietary fiber, folic acid, iron, magnesium, and vitamin B_6. In energy balls, chickpeas contribute a moist, soft texture, and add bulk. The best variety to use are organic canned chickpeas that contain no additives or preservatives.

Hazelnuts

Hazelnuts, also known as filberts, are incredibly nutritious and have a flavor that works well with many foods, including chocolate. The raw nuts are loaded with vitamin E, which has been shown to help prevent damage from endurance exercise. Just 3 Tbsp of raw hazelnuts contain 3 g of dietary fiber and ample amounts of unsaturated fats and magnesium. Along with their delicious flavor, these nuts add flavor, crunch, and bulk to energy balls.

Hemp Seeds

Hemp seeds and hemp hearts (which are shelled hemp seeds) come from the hemp plant, which is part of the cannabis family—but don't be alarmed; they won't alter your mood or state of mind. The seeds are loaded with protein, which makes them a fantastic performance booster. And that's not all—they are also rich in fiber, essential fatty acids, iron, magnesium, and potassium as well as antioxidants, including vitamin E. In energy balls, hemp seeds add bulk and a nutty flavor. They work well as a coating, too.

Hazelnuts

Sea Salt

Sea salt is exactly what it says it is: salt from the sea. Sea salt is not processed as intensely as table salt, and therefore retains many minerals that support muscle and skeletal health, as well as sodium, an electrolyte important for physical activity and enhancing performance. In small doses, salt is vital for an active individual. In energy balls, sea salt adds minerals and provides a wonderful taste that blends with sweet dates, nuts, and seeds. The best sea salt for the energy balls in this chapter is crystallized, not flaked, as it has a better consistency.

Vegan Protein Powder

It's no surprise that protein boosts performance, which is why vegan protein powder is such a pivotal ingredient in this chapter. It is made from a variety of sources, including hemp, brown rice, pea, soy, or blends of two or more of these. The powders are rich in amino acids, which aid muscle growth and repair. In an energy ball, protein powder increases the protein content, of course, and also provides bulk and helps to bind the dried fruits and absorb moisture. Choose a powder that has no additives or preservatives (these may be listed as "natural flavors," "gums," "maltodextrin," and "sugar") and is naturally sweetened with stevia. If you follow a soy-free diet, choose a powder that does not contain soy protein.

Hemp seeds

Pumpkin Pie

When winter is on the way, these balls will give you a tasty, seasonal pumpkin-pie fix. Not only does pumpkin taste delicious when combined with cinnamon, nutmeg, ginger, and allspice, it's also a great source of fiber, carotenoids (phytonutrients that help fight disease and assist heart health), potassium, and magnesium. Here it is combined with fiber-packed dates, supernutritious hemp seeds, and omega-rich raw cashews. The dates make these balls sweet without adding sugar, and the healthful fats from the cashews and hemp seeds make them really filling.

1 In a food processor, combine the dates, cashews, pumpkin purée, oats, and pumpkin-pie spice and process for 1 to 2 minutes, until a sticky mass forms.

2 Spread the hemp seeds on a large plate or in a baking dish. Using a tablespoon, scoop the mixture and, with clean slightly wet hands, shape the mixture into a ball between your palms.

3 Roll the ball in the hemp seeds to lightly coat, and set on a separate plate. Repeat with the remaining mixture until you have 10 balls slightly smaller than a golf ball.

4 Place the balls in the freezer to set for 30 minutes. Store in an airtight container in the refrigerator until required, then bring to room temperature before serving.

Try this!
Pumpkin Pie–Protein
Amp up the protein even more for optimal performance and recovery! Add ½ cup [60 g] vanilla vegan protein powder and 1 Tbsp unsweetened almond milk to the food processor with the ingredients.

Cranberry–Pumpkin Pie
Reduce the dates to ¾ cup [120 g] and add ¼ cup [30 g] dried cranberries to introduce some zing, as well as a charge of energy for stamina and performance.

MAKES 10 BALLS

1 cup [160 g] pitted dates

1 cup [140 g] raw cashews

¼ cup [60 g] canned pumpkin purée

¼ cup [25 g] gluten-free rolled oats

1¼ tsp pumpkin-pie spice (or a mixture of ½ tsp ground cinnamon, ¼ tsp ground nutmeg, ¼ tsp ground ginger, and ¼ tsp ground allspice)

¼ cup [30 g] raw hemp seeds

SERVING SIZE: 1 BALL

Calories	137
Protein	4 g
Fat	6 g
Carbohydrate	17 g
Sugar	10 g
Dietary fiber	2 g
Vitamins	A, C, E
Minerals	calcium, iron, magnesium, manganese

For even more pumpkin goodness, add 1 Tbsp chopped pumpkin seeds to the coating mixture.

Double-Chocolate Fudge

The rich, intense chocolate flavor in these protein-packed fudge balls will make an energizing addition to your day. Not only that, they are a great pre- or postworkout snack. This is because they are low in dietary fat, which at most times isn't an issue. However, during and after a workout, fat can slow down the body's ability to digest protein and use it for muscle growth and repair. These balls are also loaded with magnesium, potassium, calcium, iron, and manganese, which all enhance athletic performance. Fudge that does you good? You got it!

1 In a food processor, combine the coconut cream, figs, whole almonds, protein powder, almond butter, and ¼ cup [20 g] cocoa powder and process on high for 1 minute.

2 Slowly pour in the almond milk through the top opening as you continue to process the mixture at a slow speed or pulse for another 30 seconds.

3 Using a spatula, scrape the mixture into a large bowl. Let sit at room temperature for 10 minutes, until the mixture is less sticky and easier to roll into balls.

4 Using a tablespoon, scoop the mixture and, with clean slightly wet hands, shape the mixture into a ball between your palms. Set the ball on a plate. Repeat with the remaining mixture until you have 18 balls slightly smaller than a golf ball. Sprinkle the balls with the ½ tsp cocoa powder.

5 Place the balls in the freezer to set for 30 minutes. Store in an airtight container in the refrigerator until required. Bring to room temperature before serving.

Try this!

Chocolate-Chia Protein Fudge

Add a little crunch to these balls—plus beneficial omega fatty acids and fiber—by rolling them in ½ cup [80 g] white or black chia seeds. Simply spread the seeds on a plate and roll each ball in the seeds to lightly coat rather than sprinkle with cocoa powder.

MAKES 18 BALLS

½ cup [120 ml] coconut cream

½ cup [80 g] Turkish figs

½ cup [70 g] raw almonds

½ cup [60 g] chocolate vegan protein powder

¼ cup [65 g] almond butter

¼ cup [20 g] natural cocoa powder, plus ½ tsp

¼ cup [60 ml] unsweetened almond milk

SERVING SIZE: 1 BALL

Calories	79
Protein	5 g
Fat	4 g
Carbohydrate	6 g
Sugar	3 g
Dietary fiber	2 g
Vitamins	B_2, E, K
Minerals	calcium, iron, magnesium, manganese, potassium

Chocolate-Hazelnut

Chocolate and hazelnut come together to create a fudge-like snack with a tasty crunch. The nuts, dates, cocoa powder, rolled oats, maple syrup, and almond milk make for great flavor—and have energizing and performance-enhancing benefits. The hazelnuts are packed with vitamin E, which, studies say, helps prevent oxidative damage from endurance exercise. If you are a long-distance runner, the oats will give you slow-releasing stamina and protect your body at the same time.

MAKES 12 BALLS

1 cup [160 g] pitted dates

1 cup [120 g] raw hazelnuts, plus ¼ cup [35 g] chopped

½ cup [50 g] gluten-free rolled oats

¼ cup [20 g] natural cocoa powder

3 Tbsp pure maple syrup

2 Tbsp unsweetened almond milk

1 In a food processor, combine the dates, whole hazelnuts, oats, cocoa powder, and maple syrup and process on high for 1 minute.

2 Slowly pour in the almond milk through the top opening as you continue to process the mixture at a slow speed or pulse until a sticky mass forms.

3 Spread the chopped hazelnuts on a plate. Using a tablespoon, scoop the mixture and, with clean slightly wet hands, shape the mixture into a ball between your palms.

4 Roll the ball in the chopped hazelnuts to lightly coat, and set on a plate. Repeat with the remaining mixture until you have 12 balls, each just smaller than a golf ball.

5 Place the balls in the freezer to set for 30 minutes. Store in an airtight container in the refrigerator until required. Bring to room temperature before serving.

SERVING SIZE: 1 BALL	
Calories	146
Protein	3 g
Fat	8 g
Carbohydrate	18 g
Sugar	11 g
Dietary fiber	3 g
Vitamins	all B's, E, K
Minerals	calcium, magnesium, manganese, zinc

Try this!
Chocolate-Hazelnut-Protein
Up the protein content to make these balls even more beneficial for muscle growth and repair. Reduce the cocoa powder to 2 Tbsp, add ½ cup [60 g] chocolate vegan protein powder, and increase the almond milk to ⅓ cup [80 ml].

Hemp, Hazelnut, and Chocolate
You can also use hemp seeds to add protein. Add ¼ cup [30 g] hemp seeds to the food processor with the rest of the ingredients. To coat the balls, replace the ¼ cup [35 g] chopped hazelnuts with a mixture of 2 Tbsp hemp seeds and 2 Tbsp chopped hazelnuts.

Apricot and Cashew

A delicious mix of apricots, cashews, coconut, oats, coconut nectar, hemp seeds, sea salt, and coconut milk means these balls are as easy to eat as they are simple to make. Apricots are a source of vitamin A, which boosts the function of the eyes. Cashews and coconut provide dietary fats to stimulate the metabolism, while the oats are a source of B vitamins, which aid nervous system function. Hemp seeds contain protein for muscle growth and repair.

1 In a food processor, combine the apricots, coconut, cashews, oats, coconut nectar, hemp seeds, coconut milk, and sea salt and process for 1 to 2 minutes, until a sticky mass forms.

2 Using a tablespoon, scoop the mixture and, with clean slightly wet hands, shape the mixture into a ball between your palms, and set on a plate. Repeat with the remaining mixture until you have 14 balls, each just smaller than a golf ball.

3 Place the balls in the freezer to set for 30 minutes. Store in an airtight container in the refrigerator or at room temperature until required. Bring to room temperature before serving.

Try this!
Banana, Apricot, and Cashew
Add the performance-enhancing benefits of potassium-rich banana to these balls. Simply reduce the dried apricots to ½ cup [90 g] and add ½ cup [50 g] chopped dried whole banana to the food processor with the rest of the ingredients.

MAKES 14 BALLS

1 cup [180 g] dried Turkish apricots

¾ cup [75 g] unsweetened shredded coconut

½ cup [70 g] raw cashews

⅓ cup [65 g] gluten-free rolled oats

2 Tbsp coconut nectar

2 Tbsp hemp seeds

2 Tbsp unsweetened coconut milk

⅛ tsp sea salt

SERVING SIZE: 1 BALL

Calories	109
Protein	2 g
Fat	5 g
Carbohydrate	14 g
Sugar	7 g
Dietary fiber	2 g
Vitamins	A, B_6
Minerals	iron, magnesium, zinc

Always be sure to buy dried fruits that have not been treated with sulfur.

Toasted Coconut Fudge

These balls turn the concept of fudge on its head, thanks to a balance of healthy fats, protein, and carbohydrates. The dates, almonds, cocoa, almond butter, maple syrup, coconut, and almond milk make a great taste combination, and toasting the coconut really adds to the flavor. These balls are rich in vitamins and minerals to help prevent muscle damage, aid speed and agility, and support muscle and bone health.

MAKES 16 BALLS

¼ cup [20 g] unsweetened coconut flakes

1 cup [160 g] pitted dates

1 cup [140 g] raw almonds

¼ cup [20 g] natural cocoa powder

2 Tbsp natural almond butter

2 Tbsp pure maple syrup

2 Tbsp unsweetened shredded coconut

2 Tbsp unsweetened almond milk

1 Place the coconut flakes in a skillet and cook over medium heat for 2 minutes, or until lightly browned. Keep a close eye on the pan and stir occasionally to be sure the coconut doesn't burn. Transfer to a bowl and let cool.

2 In a food processor, combine the dates, almonds, cocoa powder, almond butter, maple syrup, and shredded coconut and process on high for 1 minute. Slowly pour in the almond milk through the top opening as you continue to process at a slow speed or pulse until a sticky mass forms.

3 Place the cooled toasted coconut flakes in a ziplock food bag and use a rolling pin or mallet to crush the coconut into small pieces. Spread the coconut on a plate.

4 Using a tablespoon, scoop the mixture and, with clean slightly wet hands, shape the mixture into a ball between your palms. Roll the ball in the toasted coconut to lightly coat, and set on a separate plate. Repeat with the remaining mixture until you have 16 balls, each just smaller than a golf ball. Place the balls in the freezer to set for 30 minutes. Store in an airtight container in the refrigerator until required.

SERVING SIZE: 1 BALL	
Calories	114
Protein	3 g
Fat	7 g
Carbohydrate	12 g
Sugar	8 g
Dietary fiber	2 g
Vitamins	B₂, E
Minerals	copper, iron, magnesium, manganese, zinc

Try this!

Toasted Coconut and Peanut Butter
Omit the almond butter and add 2 Tbsp natural peanut butter to the food processor with the remaining ingredients.

Toasted Coconut and Cherry Fudge
Reduce the dates to ½ cup [80 g] and add ½ cup [60 g] dried unsweetened cherries.

Cookie Dough

The sweet, fudgy taste of cookie dough has always been a favorite of mine, and takes me back to my childhood when I would get to "lick the spoon!" While that cookie dough wasn't that healthy, these energy-boosting balls sure are. Amino acids from the protein powder aid muscle growth and repair; slow-release carbohydrates from the oats bring energy that lasts; plus there are healthy fats from the nuts. The ingredients also contain iron, which increases aerobic capacity, giving the body the ability to do more aerobic activity for longer.

1 In a food processor, combine the cashews, oats, almond meal, protein powder, and cashew butter and process on high for 1 to 2 minutes, until a crumbly mass forms.

2 Slowly pour the maple syrup and almond milk through the top opening as you continue to process the mixture. Add the dates and process at slow speed or pulse for 1 to 2 minutes, until a thick mixture forms. Transfer the mixture to a large bowl and fold in the chocolate chips.

3 Using a teaspoon, scoop the mixture and, with clean slightly wet hands, shape the mixture into a ball between your palms. Set the ball on a plate. Repeat with the remaining mixture until you have 20 balls, each about the size of a large marble.

4 Place the balls in the freezer to set for 30 minutes. Store in an airtight container in the refrigerator or at room temperature until required.

Try this!

Peanut Butter Cookie Dough

Try a different flavor by adding peanuts and peanut butter, which are both rich in magnesium and vitamin B_6. Omit the cashews and cashew butter and replace with ½ cup [70 g] raw shelled peanuts and 2 Tbsp natural peanut butter.

Goji Berry Cookie Dough

Goji berries increase maximum oxygen uptake and endurance, and decrease fatigue for better stamina. Simply fold in 2 Tbsp chopped dried goji berries along with the dark chocolate chips.

MAKES 20 BALLS

½ cup [70 g] raw cashews

½ cup [50 g] gluten-free rolled oats

¼ cup [30 g] almond meal or flour or ground almonds

¼ cup [30 g] vanilla vegan protein powder

2 Tbsp cashew butter

2 Tbsp pure maple syrup

2 Tbsp unsweetened almond milk

10 pitted dates

2 Tbsp mini dark chocolate chips

SERVING SIZE: 2 MINI BALLS	
Calories	136
Protein	5 g
Fat	6 g
Carbohydrate	16 g
Sugar	8 g
Dietary fiber	2 g
Vitamins	A, all B's, K
Minerals	iron, magnesium, manganese, phosphorus

MAKES 12 BALLS

¾ cup [90 g] almond meal
or ground almonds

½ cup [80 g] pitted dates

¼ cup [35 g] dark raisins

¼ cup [45 g] dried
unsweetened pineapple

¼ cup [30 g] raw
walnut halves

1 cup [90 g] peeled and
shredded carrots

½ cup [50 g] unsweetened
shredded coconut

1 heaping tsp ground cinnamon,
plus more for sprinkling

¼ tsp ground nutmeg

¼ tsp ground cardamom

FOR THE ICING
1 Tbsp vanilla vegan
protein powder

2 Tbsp unsweetened
almond milk

½ tsp melted coconut oil

1 drop pure vanilla extract

SERVING SIZE: 1 BALL	
Calories	129
Protein	4 g
Fat	7 g
Carbohydrate	15 g
Sugar	9 g
Dietary fiber	3 g
Vitamins	A, B₂, B₆, C, E
Minerals	copper, magnesium, manganese, phosphorus, potassium

Carrot Cake

These carrot cake balls help to increase energy levels for optimal mental and physical performance. They contain almonds, walnuts, raisins, dried pineapple, dates, shredded carrot, coconut, and those classic carrot cake spices: cinnamon, nutmeg, and cardamom. These ingredients bring vitamins A, C, and E—powerful antioxidants that aid immune function and exercise recovery time—as well as minerals that support muscle and bone health. The icing is the perfect finishing touch, as it is loaded with protein for performance and a delicious vanilla flavor!

1 In a food processor, combine the almond meal, dates, raisins, pineapple, walnuts, and 1 Tbsp water and process for 1 minute, or until everything is incorporated. Add the carrots, coconut, cinnamon, nutmeg, and cardamom and process again for 1 to 2 minutes, until a sticky mass forms.

2 Using a tablespoon, scoop the mixture and, with clean slightly wet hands, shape the mixture into a ball between your palms, and set on a plate. Repeat with the remaining mixture until you have 12 balls, each just smaller than a golf ball. Place the balls in the freezer to set.

3 Meanwhile, make the icing. Place the protein powder in a small bowl and pour in the almond milk, melted coconut oil, and vanilla, stirring until the icing is the consistency of heavy cream.

4 Remove the balls from the freezer and spoon about ½ tsp of the icing onto the top of each one. It will run slightly, but should not run off the balls. Sprinkle a pinch of cinnamon on the top of each ball and return to the freezer for 1 hour to set. Store in an airtight container in the freezer until required (the icing will become soft if stored in the refrigerator or at room temperature).

Try this!
Naked Carrot Cake
Not into the protein icing? No problem! Just omit the icing and enjoy the simply delicious carrot cake flavor on its own.

Bring a citrus burst to these balls by sprinkling the icing with a little finely grated orange zest.

Vanilla Cake

Moist, fluffy, and cakelike, these balls are a treat to enjoy at any time of the day or whenever your performance needs a helping hand. The secret ingredient is the humble chickpea, which adds energy-giving complex carbohydrates and protein, as well as contributing to the moist, soft texture. Vanilla protein powder provides amino acids for muscle growth and repair, while the coconut butter and cashews bring in some nice healthy fats. Who says you can't have your cake and eat it too?

1 Combine the chickpeas, coconut nectar, protein powder, almond flour, coconut butter, cashew butter, vanilla, and salt in a food processor and process for 1 to 2 minutes, until a smooth mass forms. You may need to scrape down the sides of the bowl from time to time to ensure all the ingredients are incorporated.

2 Spread the sprinkles on a plate.

3 Using a tablespoon, scoop the mixture and, with clean slightly wet hands, shape the mixture into a ball between your palms. Roll the ball in the sprinkles to lightly coat, and set on a separate plate. Repeat with the remaining mixture until you have 16 balls slightly smaller than a golf ball.

4 Place the balls in the freezer to set for 30 minutes. Store in an airtight container in the refrigerator until required.

Try this!

Chocolate-Coated Vanilla Cake

Vanilla and chocolate is a classic flavor combination, and dark chocolate is a great source of antioxidants. To coat these balls in chocolate, omit the sprinkles or shredded coconut. Melt ¼ cup [45 g] chopped 70 percent cacao solids vegan dark chocolate with 1 tsp coconut oil in a small saucepan over low heat, stirring until smooth. Remove from the heat. Freeze the balls for 30 minutes, then place one on the tip of a skewer or toothpick. Dip it in the melted chocolate to coat it, then lift it out and rotate it while the chocolate sets. Set the ball on a clean plate and repeat with the remaining balls. Return the balls to the freezer for 30 minutes to 1 hour. Store in an airtight container in the refrigerator until required.

MAKES 16 BALLS

1½ cups [300 g] canned chickpeas, drained and rinsed

¼ cup [60 ml] coconut or agave nectar

¼ cup [30 g] vanilla vegan protein powder

2 Tbsp almond flour or meal or ground almonds

2 Tbsp coconut butter

2 Tbsp cashew butter

½ tsp vanilla powder or pure vanilla extract

pinch of salt

½ cup [80 g] vegan sprinkles or ½ cup [50 g] unsweetened shredded coconut

SERVING SIZE: 1 BALL	
Calories	99
Protein	3 g
Fat	3 g
Carbohydrate	16 g
Sugar	12 g
Dietary fiber	1 g
Vitamins	B_1, B_6, K
Minerals	copper, iron, magnesium, manganese, phosphorus

Sprinkles
or coconut make a
great coating for these
balls, but you can also try
shaved dark chocolate
or chopped nuts.

Salted Caramel and Chia

When dates are combined with cashew butter, almond milk, maple syrup, and chia seeds it creates a delicious caramel flavor. And you can enhance it by adding a little sea salt. The salt is rich in minerals that support muscle and skeletal health, as well as sodium, an electrolyte important for physical activity. The dates contain carbohydrates, which provide a perfect hit of energy, while the chia seeds bring healthy fats, protein, and fiber.

MAKES 14 BALLS

1 cup [160 g] pitted dates

1 Tbsp chia seeds, plus 3 Tbsp

¼ tsp sea salt

2 Tbsp cashew butter

1 Tbsp unsweetened almond milk

1 Tbsp pure maple syrup

1 cup [140 g] raw almonds

1 Combine the dates and 1 Tbsp chai seeds in a heatproof bowl and pour over ½ cup [120 ml] boiling water. Add the sea salt and mix so that everything is moistened. Let the dates and chia soak for 10 minutes, until all of the water is absorbed.

2 Transfer the soaked date mixture to a food processor. Add the cashew butter, almond milk, and maple syrup and process for 1 to 2 minutes, until a thick mass forms. Transfer the mixture to a bowl and set aside.

3 Put the almonds in the food processor and process for 1 to 2 minutes, until a crumbly flour forms. Return the date mixture to the processor and process for 30 seconds, until combined. Return the mixture to the bowl and freeze for about 15 minutes to set.

4 Place the 3 Tbsp chia seeds on a plate. Using a tablespoon, scoop the mixture and, with clean slightly wet hands, shape the mixture into a ball between your palms. Roll the ball in the chia seeds to lightly coat, and set on a separate plate. Repeat with the remaining mixture until you have 14 balls slightly smaller than a golf ball.

5 Place the balls in the freezer to set for 30 minutes. Store in an airtight container in the freezer or refrigerator until required.

Try this!

Salted Caramel and Hazelnuts

Hazelnuts are a great source of vitamin C, which helps boost immunity and, as a result, performance. Plus their flavor combines well with caramel. Omit the 3 Tbsp chia seeds for the coating and replace with ½ cup [70 g] crushed raw hazelnuts.

SERVING SIZE: 1 BALL	
Calories	113
Protein	3 g
Fat	6 g
Carbohydrate	13 g
Sugar	9 g
Dietary fiber	2 g
Vitamins	B_2, B_6, E
Minerals	magnesium, manganese, potassium, sodium

[Bedtime]
Energy Balls

These luscious, sweet, and appetizing recipes are designed to meet all of your bedtime energy needs. They are filled with healthy ingredients, such as citrus fruits, cherries, and cranberries, which are rich in antioxidants; spices like chili and ginger that will rev up your libido; omega-rich pistachios; and special superfoods such as maca root powder. These ingredients provide an evening dose of nutrients that will either boost your libido or promote rest and relaxation . . . what a perfect way to end the day!

Active Ingredients

Cherries

Dried, unsweetened Bing cherries are the best cherry option for energy balls, as they are sweeter than other varieties and provide a robust cherry flavor. Dried cherries are a source of copper and vitamins A and C. They are also known to have an aphrodisiac effect, as they have been said to stimulate pheromone production. In energy balls, dried cherries add a soft and chewy texture, work as a sticky binding ingredient, and add a sweet and slightly tart flavor. Look for natural, unsulfured, unsweetened varieties.

Cranberries

Dried cranberries are partially dehydrated fresh berries. Most dried cranberries have been sweetened, so look for brands that use natural sweeteners such as fruit juice. It is possible to find unsweetened dried cranberries, and these work well in energy balls, too, although the finished balls will be less sweet. Dried cranberries are a good source of antioxidants including vitamin C, which boosts adrenal function, and vitamins B_3, E, and K. Dried cranberries add a slightly tart taste, a soft and chewy consistency, and work as a sticky binding ingredient in energy balls.

Cranberries

Ginger

Ground ginger is made by peeling and drying the fresh root, then grinding it into a fine powder. The pungent flavor is refreshing and almost citrusy. It is a natural antibacterial and anti-inflammatory, and has also been known to increase libido. Ginger is also a source of the mineral manganese. In energy balls, the flavor combines well with fruits such as pear and mango. If you wish to use fresh grated ginger root, substitute the same amount as ground ginger for a more subtle ginger taste.

Limes

This tasty, sweet, and tart fruit is rich in antioxidants and bursting with vitamin C. Like oranges, the vitamin C found in limes helps to boost the adrenal glands. These glands regulate some of the hormones that help promote a deep restful sleep, making limes a great bedtime addition. Limes are typically used for their juice and rind. In energy balls, lime juice and zest add a wonderful citrus flavor and moisture.

Maca Powder

The root of the maca plant is dried and ground to make a powder in the same way as ginger. It has multiple health benefits, including the ability to naturally aid libido and balance hormones. At bedtime, maca powder is a perfect addition for that aphrodisiac effect. It is also rich in amino acids, B vitamins, and a multitude of minerals. In energy balls, maca powder adds a slightly smoky flavor and blends with ginger and mango.

Oranges

Oranges are a delicious member of the citrus family. This juicy fruit is rich in antioxidants and bursting with vitamin C. Natural orange juice is recommended in the evening as part of an "adrenal cocktail" to help boost the adrenal glands, which regulate some of the hormones needed to promote a deep, restful sleep. In energy balls, the juice and zest provide vitamin C, a burst of orange flavor, and lend moisture to help bind the other ingredients.

Pistachios

Pistachios are rich in nutrients, including healthy unsaturated fats, B vitamins, phosphorus, manganese, iron, and copper. These nuts have also been known to boost sleep quality, as they are rich in vitamin B_6, which helps to produce the relaxation-promoting hormone serotonin. Pistachios add a crunchy texture and bulk to energy balls. Crushed pistachios make a fantastic ball coating, too.

Red Pepper (Chili) Flakes

Red pepper flakes are made from red chile peppers that have been dried and then crushed into flakes rather than ground. These peppers, and their dried flakes, have been known to be a natural aphrodisiac, as they increase circulation in the body. Red pepper flakes are also a great source of vitamin A. Because the flakes are so spicy, a little goes a long way. Use sparingly to get that circulation going and raise the temperature in the bedroom!

Oranges

Pistachios

Cashew, Cranberry, and Coconut

Cranberries are reputed to be a natural aphrodisiac, but they also increase immunity and have antioxidant properties. These energy balls are bursting with dried cranberries combined with raw cashews, dates, coconut, vanilla protein powder, and almond milk. The magnesium in the cashews and coconut helps to encourage a deeper, more restful sleep, while the protein powder provides tryptophan, an amino acid that is also a natural sleep aid and mood enhancer. This tasty combination is sure to put you in the right frame of mind for bedtime!

MAKES 18 BALLS

1 cup [160 g] pitted dates

1 cup [140 g] raw cashews

½ cup [60 g] dried cranberries

½ cup [60 g] vanilla vegan protein powder

½ cup [50 g] unsweetened shredded coconut, plus 2 Tbsp

2 Tbsp unsweetened almond milk

1 In a food processor, combine the dates, cashews, cranberries, protein powder, and ½ cup [50 g] coconut and process for 3 minutes, until you have a crumbly, well incorporated consistency. Add 1 Tbsp of the almond milk and process for another 1 to 2 minutes, until the mixture is sticky enough to roll into balls. If the mixture is still too crumbly, add the remaining 1 Tbsp almond milk and process for another 1 to 2 minutes.

2 Spread the 2 Tbsp shredded coconut on a large plate.

3 Using a tablespoon, scoop the mixture and, with clean slightly wet hands, shape the mixture into a ball between your palms. Roll the ball in the coconut to lightly coat, and set on a separate plate. Repeat with the remaining mixture until you have 18 balls slightly smaller than a golf ball.

4 Place the balls in the freezer to set for 1 to 2 hours. Store in an airtight container in the refrigerator until required.

Try this!

Cashew, Cranberry, and Apple

Omit the shredded coconut and protein powder. Add 1 cup [60 g] dried apple rings, 1 Tbsp unsweetened applesauce, and ½ cup [60 g] almond flour or ground almonds to the food processor with the rest of the ingredients.

SERVING SIZE: 1 BALL	
Calories	102
Protein	4 g
Fat	5 g
Carbohydrate	12 g
Sugar	8 g
Dietary fiber	1 g
Vitamins	C, E
Minerals	calcium, magnesium, manganese

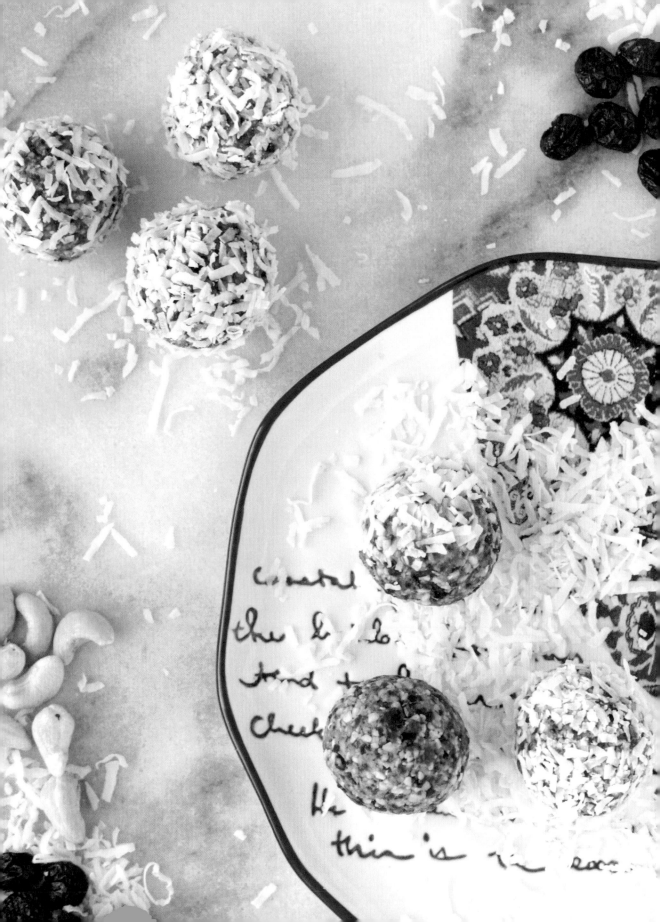

Ginger, Pear, and Pistachio

Sweet pear, crunchy pistachios, and aromatic ginger make a unique and delicious combination in these simple love life-enhancing bedtime balls. Ginger will spice things up in the bedroom, as it naturally improves circulation and blood flow. Pears are rich in vitamins C and E, which aid the immune system, and pistachios are an excellent source of vitamin B_6, which helps the body enhance its natural production of the feel-good hormone serotonin.

MAKES 18 BALLS

1 cup [160 g] pitted dates

1 cup [60 g] dried pears

½ cup [70 g] raw cashews

½ cup [70 g] raw pistachios, plus ½ cup [80 g] coarsely chopped

½ cup [50 g] gluten-free quick oats

1 Tbsp cashew butter

2 tsp ground ginger

1 In a food processor, combine the dates, pears, cashews, whole pistachios, oats, cashew butter, ginger, and 3 Tbsp water and process on high speed for 2 to 3 minutes, until a thick, sticky mass forms. You may need to add another 2 to 3 Tbsp water.

2 Spread the chopped pistachios on a large plate.

3 Using a tablespoon, scoop the mixture and, with clean slightly wet hands, shape the mixture into a ball between your palms. Roll the ball in the chopped pistachios to lightly coat, and set on a separate plate. Repeat with the remaining mixture until you have 18 balls slightly smaller than a golf ball.

4 Place the balls in the freezer to set for 30 minutes. Store in an airtight container in the refrigerator or at room temperature until required.

Try this!

Spiced Ginger–Pear

Omit the whole and crushed pistachios and increase the cashews to 1 cup [140 g]. Add 2 tsp ground cinnamon to the ingredients before you process them for a spicy touch!

SERVING SIZE: 1 BALL	
Calories	120
Protein	3 g
Fat	5 g
Carbohydrate	17 g
Sugar	8 g
Dietary fiber	3 g
Vitamins	B_6, C, E
Minerals	calcium, magnesium

Chocolate-Orange

Citrus and chocolate are a match made in heaven, so move over mint and peanut butter—orange is here to stay! Orange is high in vitamin C, which gives the adrenal glands a helping hand. The adrenals regulate and manage the effect of stress on the body, and a dose of vitamin C helps the body to deal with stress. Dark chocolate contains antioxidants that increase immunity and combat disease, and dates are a great source of calcium, which has a naturally calming effect.

MAKES 15 BALLS

1 cup [160 g] pitted dates

1 cup [140 g] raw cashews

¼ cup [25 g] coconut flour

¼ cup [60 ml] fresh orange juice, plus 4 Tbsp finely grated zest

½ cup [100 g] chopped 70% cacao dark chocolate

1 Tbsp coconut oil

SERVING SIZE: 1 BALL	
Calories	127
Protein	2 g
Fat	7 g
Carbohydrate	14 g
Sugar	9 g
Dietary fiber	2 g
Vitamins	B₆, C, E
Minerals	calcium, magnesium

1 In a food processor, combine the dates, cashews, coconut flour, orange juice, and 2 Tbsp of the orange zest and process for 2 to 3 minutes, until a sticky mass forms.

2 Using a tablespoon, scoop the mixture and, with clean slightly wet hands, shape the mixture into a ball between your palms. Set the ball on a plate. Repeat with the remaining mixture until you have 15 balls, each about the size of a golf ball. Place the balls in the freezer to set for 1 hour.

3 Meanwhile, combine the chocolate and coconut oil in a saucepan over low heat and cook, stirring until melted and smooth. Remove from the heat. Sprinkle the remaining 2 Tbsp zest onto a plate.

4 Secure one of the frozen balls on the end of a toothpick or skewer. Holding the toothpick, roll the ball in the melted chocolate until it is coated, then lift it out, and place on a separate plate. Sprinkle with a little of the zest. Repeat with the remaining balls.

5 Return the balls to the freezer for another 30 minutes to set. Store in an airtight container in the refrigerator until required.

Try this!

Orange and Maca

Omit the chocolate and orange coating. Reduce the coconut flour to 3½ Tbsp and add ½ Tbsp maca root powder for a libido boost!

Chocolate-Orange Fudge

Add ¼ cup [20 g] natural cocoa powder to the ingredients, and increase the orange juice to ½ cup [120 ml]. Process the mixture for slightly longer, until you have a smooth, fudgelike consistency. Coat the balls with chocolate and orange zest as directed.

Chocolate–Almond Truffles

One of my favorite ways to end the day is to sit down with some antioxidant-rich dark chocolate. But when there isn't any chocolate around, these chocolate–almond truffle balls definitely do the trick. Each one has a rich and comforting chocolaty flavor, balanced out with ample protein from both the protein powder and the almonds to aid relaxation. The almonds are also rich in the sleep-promoting amino acid tryptophan.

MAKES 30 BALLS

1 cup [140 g] raw almonds

1 cup [120 g] chocolate vegan protein powder

1 cup [100 g] gluten-free rolled oats

3 Tbsp natural cocoa powder, plus 2 Tbsp

1 cup [160 g] pitted dates

3 Tbsp unsweetened almond milk

1 In a food processor, combine the almonds, protein powder, oats, and 3 Tbsp cocoa powder and process for 30 seconds.

2 Add the dates and while you continue to process, slowly pour in the almond milk until the mixture starts to clump together, for 1 to 2 minutes.

3 Line a baking sheet with parchment paper. Using a tablespoon measure, scoop out the mixture and, with clean slightly wet hands, shape the mixture into a ball between your palms. Place on the prepared baking sheet. Repeat with the remaining mixture until you have 30 balls slightly smaller than a golf ball.

4 Sprinkle the balls with the 2 Tbsp cocoa powder and roll until they are all lightly coated.

5 Place the balls in the freezer for 30 minutes to set. Store in an airtight container in the refrigerator or at room temperature until required.

SERVING SIZE: 1 BALL	
Calories	83
Protein	4 g
Fat	3 g
Carbohydrate	13 g
Sugar	6 g
Dietary fiber	–
Vitamins	B_2, E
Minerals	calcium, magnesium, zinc

Try this!

Chocolate–Lavender Truffles

Introduce the calming, relaxing effect of lavender to these bedtime balls by adding a heaping 1 Tbsp of dried food-grade lavender buds or ½ tsp pure lavender extract to the food processor with the dates and almond milk.

Sift the cocoa powder before you use it to remove any lumps.

Double-Chocolate and Cherry

Delicious cherries are a natural sleep promoter, as they are rich in melatonin, which helps you to sleep well. These indulgent bedtime balls combine tart, unsweetened cherries with other sleep-promoting foods—almonds, almond milk, cocoa powder, and chocolate protein powder. The protein powder contains amino acids that promote muscle repair and relaxation, while the almond milk and almonds supply the mood-boosting amino acid tryptophan, and cocoa powder contains magnesium, the great sleep-promoting mineral.

1 In a food processor, combine the almonds, protein powder, and 2 Tbsp cocoa powder and blend for 30 seconds.

2 Add the dates, cherries, and almond milk and process for 1 to 2 minutes, until the mixture is well combined. Once a sticky, smooth mass forms, scrape it into a large bowl.

3 Sprinkle the 2 tsp cocoa powder on a plate. Using a tablespoon, scoop out a 2-Tbsp portion of the mixture and, with clean slightly wet hands, shape the mixture into a ball between your palms. Roll the ball in the cocoa powder until it is lightly coated, and set on a separate plate. Repeat with the remaining mixture until you have 15 balls slightly smaller than a golf ball.

4 Store in an airtight container in the refrigerator until required. Bring to room temperature before serving.

MAKES 15 BALLS

1 cup [140 g] raw almonds

½ cup [60 g] chocolate vegan protein powder

2 Tbsp natural cocoa powder, plus 2 tsp

1 cup [160 g] pitted dates

1 cup [120 g] dried unsweetened cherries

2 Tbsp unsweetened almond milk

SERVING SIZE: 1 BALL	
Calories	90
Protein	5 g
Fat	3 g
Carbohydrate	12 g
Sugar	8 g
Dietary fiber	3 g
Vitamins	A, C
Minerals	calcium, magnesium, potassium

Try this!

Chocolate, Macadamia, and Cherry

Omit the almonds and replace them with 1 cup [125 g] raw macadamia nuts, another deep-sleep promoter. Omit the cocoa powder coating and let the macadamia flavor shine.

Vanilla and Cherry

Omit the cocoa powder. Replace the chocolate protein powder with ½ cup [60 g] vanilla vegan protein powder and add 1 tsp pure vanilla extract to the ingredients before processing.

If necessary, scrape down the sides of the food processor bowl with a spatula every 20 seconds to ensure all the ingredients are incorporated.

Lime and Coconut

Craving some refreshing tropical flavors? These delicious balls contain vitamin C from the lime, which enhances immune function and serotonin production. Enjoying some vitamin C at bedtime is especially helpful, as it may improve the brain chemistry that is essential for restful sleep. Along with the benefits of the lime, these balls are loaded with coconut, which is high in fiber, selenium, and vitamin B_6—also known as pyridoxine—which helps the body produce more serotonin for a sound night's sleep.

MAKES 12 BALLS

½ cup [60 g] almond meal or ground almonds

½ cup [50 g] coconut flour

½ cup [50 g] unsweetened shredded coconut, plus 2 Tbsp

2 Tbsp pure maple syrup

2 Tbsp fresh lime juice, plus 2 tsp finely grated zest

1 Tbsp unsweetened almond milk

10 pitted dates

1 In a food processor, combine the almond meal, coconut flour, ½ cup [50 g] coconut, maple syrup, lime juice, almond milk, and 1 tsp of the lime zest and process for 1 to 2 minutes, until a crumbly mass forms. Add the dates and process for 30 seconds to 1 minute, until a sticky but slightly crumbly mass forms.

2 In a small bowl, stir together the 2 Tbsp shredded coconut and remaining 1 tsp lime zest, then spread on a large plate.

3 Using a tablespoon, scoop the mixture and, with clean slightly wet hands, shape the mixture into a ball between your palms. Roll the ball in the coconut and zest mixture to lightly coat, and set on a separate plate. Repeat with the remaining mixture until you have 12 balls, each slightly smaller than a golf ball.

4 Place the balls in the freezer to set for 30 minutes. Store in an airtight container in the refrigerator until required.

Try this!

Chocolate-Coated Lime

Adding dark chocolate to these balls should perk up your love life. While the shaped balls set in the freezer, combine ¼ cup [45 g] chopped dark chocolate and ½ Tbsp coconut oil in a saucepan over low heat and cook, stirring until melted and smooth. Remove from the heat. Place one of the frozen balls on the end of a skewer or toothpick. Holding the skewer, roll the ball in the melted chocolate mixture until it is coated. Lift it out and place on a plate. Repeat with the remaining balls. Return the balls to the freezer for another 30 minutes to set.

SERVING SIZE: 1 BALL	
Calories	101
Protein	2 g
Fat	5 g
Carbohydrate	12 g
Sugar	8 g
Dietary fiber	3 g
Vitamins	B_2, B_6, C, E
Minerals	magnesium, manganese, phosphorus, selenium

Ginger and Graham Cracker Crumble

Spicy ginger, aromatic cinnamon, rich molasses, sweet dates, chewy raisins, and fiber-rich oats come together in these gingerbread-inspired energy balls, while a sweet and crunchy graham cracker coating adds more taste and texture. Ginger has libido-maximizing benefits, as it gets the blood flowing around the body. Along with the ginger, cinnamon is a natural aphrodisiac, and the molasses brings magnesium, which will help you to relax and—when you are ready—to fall into a deep and satisfying sleep.

MAKES 16 BALLS

1½ cups [180 g] walnut halves

¾ cup [75 g] gluten-free quick oats

1 Tbsp ground cinnamon

2 tsp ground ginger

1 tsp ground nutmeg

1 cup [160 g] pitted dates

½ cup [70 g] dark raisins

1 Tbsp organic blackstrap molasses

1 Tbsp pure maple syrup

½ cup [40 g] gluten-free graham cracker crumbs [about 4 crackers]

1 In a food processor, combine the walnuts, oats, cinnamon, ginger, and nutmeg and process until finely ground. Add the dates and raisins and process again for 1 minute.

2 Slowly pour the molasses and maple syrup through the top opening as you continue to process the mixture and a sticky mass forms. If it seems too dry, add 1 Tbsp water and process again until sticky.

3 Spread the graham cracker crumbs on a plate. Using a tablespoon, scoop the mixture and, with clean slightly wet hands, shape the mixture into a ball between your palms.

4 Roll the ball in the cracker crumbs to lightly coat, and set on a separate plate. Repeat with the remaining mixture until you have 16 balls, each slightly smaller than a golf ball.

5 Place the balls in the freezer to set for 1 hour. Store in an airtight container in the refrigerator or freezer until required. Defrost, if necessary, and bring to room temperature before serving.

Try this!

Ginger–Pumpkin Seed

Pumpkin seeds are fantastic for prostate health and contain great love life–enhancing nutrients, plus a dose of tryptophan for sound sleep. Omit the graham cracker crumbs and coat the balls in ¼ cup [30 g] crushed raw pumpkin seeds.

SERVING SIZE: 1 BALL	
Calories	163
Protein	3 g
Fat	8 g
Carbohydrate	20 g
Sugar	13 g
Dietary fiber	3 g
Vitamins	B₁ and 6
Minerals	calcium, folic acid, iron, magnesium, manganese, phosphorus

White Chocolate, Maple, and Chili

A white chocolate–coated truffle containing maple syrup and sprinkled with chili is enough to capture anyone's heart. Chocolate is renowned as an aphrodisiac, but it's the red pepper flakes in these balls that really turn up the heat. They contain capsaicin, which increases blood flow and puts you in the mood for love. Enjoy one of these an hour before you hit the sack and you'll be energized for all kinds of fun.

MAKES 12 BALLS

1 cup [140 g] raw cashews

¼ cup [50 g] coconut butter

¼ cup [65 g] shredded or chopped cocoa butter

3 Tbsp pure maple syrup

2 Tbsp coconut flour

2 Tbsp coconut milk

FOR THE COATING

2 Tbsp chopped cocoa butter

1 heaping Tbsp coconut butter

½ Tbsp pure maple syrup

½ tsp coconut flour

½ tsp red pepper flakes

1 Place the cashews in a bowl, cover with cold water, and let soak for at least 1 hour, or preferably overnight. Drain before using.

2 Combine the drained cashews, coconut butter, cocoa butter, maple syrup, and coconut flour in a food processor and process for 30 seconds. Pour in the coconut milk and process for about 30 seconds, until a smooth mass forms.

3 Using a tablespoon, scoop the mixture and, with clean slightly wet hands, shape the mixture into a ball between your palms, and set on a plate. Repeat with the remaining mixture until you have 12 balls slightly smaller than a golf ball. Place the balls in the freezer to set for 30 minutes.

4 To make the coating, melt the cocoa butter in a small saucepan, then pour into a bowl. Stir in the coconut butter, maple syrup, and coconut flour and set aside.

5 Remove the balls from the freezer and place one on the tip of a skewer or toothpick. Dip it in the mixture to coat, lift it out, and then sprinkle with red pepper flakes. Remove the ball from the skewer and set on a clean plate. Repeat with the remaining balls.

6 Place the balls in the freezer to set for 10 minutes. Store in an airtight container in the refrigerator until required.

SERVING SIZE: 1 BALL	
Calories	185
Protein	3 g
Fat	15 g
Carbohydrate	8 g
Sugar	3 g
Dietary fiber	1 g
Vitamins	B_1, B_6, K
Minerals	copper, magnesium, manganese, phosphorus, selenium

Try this!
Double-Chocolate Chili

Pure dark chocolate is rich in antioxidants and has a reputation as a natural aphrodisiac. Omit the 2 Tbsp chopped cocoa butter in the coating and replace it with 2 Tbsp chopped dark chocolate.

Ginger, Mango, and Maca

Mango always makes me think of tropical destinations and puts me in a great mood. These balls will transport you to a lush oasis—and may also boost your love life with the addition of maca and ginger, both known for their ability to turn up the heat in the bedroom. For bedtime bliss, these balls combine sweet mango, which is rich in vitamin C for good adrenal function, to ensure deep, restful sleep; selenium-rich coconut; and nutrient-dense cashews and macadamia nuts—another exotic delight. A great flavor combination to encourage all kinds of pleasure.

MAKES 12 BALLS

1 cup [100 g] dried unsweetened mango

½ cup [70 g] raw cashews

½ cup [60 g] raw macadamia nuts

1 cup [100 g] dried shredded coconut, plus ½ tsp

1 tsp ground ginger

2 tsp coconut or agave nectar

½ tsp maca powder

1 Place the dried mango in a heatproof bowl and cover with hot water. Let soak for 5 minutes until softened, then drain.

2 Combine the cashews and macadamia nuts in a food processor and process until a crumbly mass forms. Add the soaked mango, 1 cup [140 g] coconut, ginger, coconut nectar, and maca powder and process until a sticky mass forms.

3 Using a tablespoon, scoop the mixture and, with clean slightly wet hands, shape the mixture into a ball between your palms, and set on a plate. Repeat with the remaining mixture until you have 12 balls, each just smaller than a golf ball. Sprinkle the balls with the ½ tsp shredded coconut.

4 Place the balls in the freezer to set for 30 minutes. Store in an airtight container in the refrigerator until required.

Try this!
Dark Chocolate, Ginger, and Mango
Instead of the maca, add another delicious aphrodisiac—dark chocolate. Omit the maca from the mixture and roll the balls in ¼ cup (45 g) shaved vegan dark chocolate to lightly coat them.

SERVING SIZE: 1 BALL	
Calories	145
Protein	2 g
Fat	10 g
Carbohydrate	13 g
Sugar	8 g
Dietary fiber	2 g
Vitamins	A, B₁, B₆, C, K
Minerals	copper, magnesium, manganese, phosphorus, selenium

For a less sweet flavor, omit the coconut nectar.

Resources

Many of the ingredients used in *Energy Balls* can be found in larger supermarkets. However, if you have difficulty tracking any of them down, you should be able to find them in specialty stores such as these.

USA

Natural and Organic Foods

Fresh Thyme Farmers Market
freshthyme.com

Sprouts Farmers Market
www.sprouts.com

Trader Joe's
www.traderjoes.com

Whole Foods
www.wholefoodsmarket.com

Regular Stores with Natural and Organic Foods Sections

Albertson's
www.albertsons.com

Food Lion
www.foodlion.com

Hannaford
www.hannaford.com

Harris Teeter
www.harristeeter.com

Publix
www.publix.com

Safeway
www.safeway.com

Target
www.target.com

Wegmans
www.wegmans.com

Online

Amazon
www.amazon.com

Canada

Natural and Organic Foods

Planet Organic (Edmonton, Calgary)
planetorganic.ca

Whole Foods
(Vancouver, Edmonton, Ontario)
www.wholefoodsmarket.com

Bulk Nuts/Seeds/Dried Fruits

Bulk Barn (throughout Canada)
www.bulkbarn.ca

Regular Stores with Natural and Organic Foods Sections

Real Canadian Superstore (throughout Canada)
www.realcanadiansuperstore.ca

Save-On-Foods (British Columbia and Alberta)
www.saveonfoods.com

Sobeys (throughout Canada)
www.sobeys.com

Online

Amazon
www.amazon.ca

Spud
www.spud.ca (Vancouver, Calgary, Edmonton)

Vitamart
www.vitamart.ca

UK

Natural and Organic Foods

Grape Tree
www.grapetree.co.uk

Holland & Barrett
www.hollandandbarrett.com

Planet Organic
www.planetorganic.com

Whole Foods
www.wholefoodsmarket.com

Online

Amazon
www.amazon.co.uk

Australia

Natural and Organic Foods

Fundies Wholefood Market
www.fundies.com.au

Bulk Nuts/Seeds/Dried Fruits

The Source Bulk Foods
thesourcebulkfoods.com.au

Online

Amazon
www.amazon.com.au

Aussie Health Products
www.aussiehealthproducts.com.au

Honest to Goodness
www.goodness.com.au

New Zealand

Natural and Organic Foods

Piko Wholefoods
www.pikowholefoods.co.nz

Online

Naturally Organic
www.naturallyorganic.co.nz

Index

Acknowledgments

To all of the Nutritionist in the Kitch readers who inspire and drive me to continue creating and thinking outside of the box. To my family for being my number one fans, encouraging me every step of the way. And to my husband, who ate his weight in energy balls during the making of this book, for his constant love and support.

Picture Credits

t = top; **b** = bottom

All images copyright Christal Sczebel except:

8 Food and Drink/SuperStock; **9t** Westend61/SuperStock; **9b** Westend61/SuperStock; **10t** Tetra Images/SuperStock; **10b** Food and Drink/SuperStock; **16** Westend61/SuperStock; **17t** Brian Yarvin/Alamy Stock Photo; **17b** Westend61/SuperStock; **38** Food and Drink/SuperStock; **39t** tim gartside/Alamy Stock Photo; **39b** Gerard Lacz Images/SuperStock; **60** Westend61/SuperStock; **61t** Westend61/SuperStock; **61b** Westend61/SuperStock; **82** Magdalena Niemczyk-ElanArt/SuperStock; **83t** Phanie / Phanie/SuperStock; **83b** Food and Drinks Photos/Food and Drink/SuperStock; **104** MAURITIUS/mauritius/SuperStock; **105t** Jana Ihle/Mauritius/SuperStock; **105b** Chris Warren/Food and Drink/SuperStock